Thames & Hudson

TOTAL OFFICE DESIGN

50 CONTEMPORARY WORKPLACES

Kerstin Zumstein & Helen Parton

For my daughter Mariella, who was born in the process of writing this book, and my mother Kathleen. Special thanks go to my husband for his endless support.
Kerstin Zumstein

I would like to dedicate this book to my Mum and Dad and my fantastic friends for giving me the love and support to see it through.
Helen Parton

Page 1: S11 office by Jürgen Mayer H.
Pages 2–3: PostPanic office by Maurice Mentjens Design.
Right: Gummo office by i29.

First published in the United Kingdom in 2011 by Thames & Hudson Ltd, 181A High Holborn, London WC1V 7QX

British Library Cataloguing-in-Publication Data
A catalogue record for this book is available from the British Library

ISBN 978-0-500-51586-0

Printed and bound in China by C&C Offset Printing Co Ltd

To find out about all our publications, please visit
www.thamesandhudson.com.
There you can subscribe to our e-newsletter, browse

INTRODUCTION 6

SMALL 10

MEDIUM 82

LARGE 188

Introduction

Architecture and, in particular, workplace design, have undergone great change since the recession struck in 2008. A much closer check on budgets, as well as heightened levels of accountability for ecological design decisions, are shaping a new office model.

Although certain elements, such as break-out areas, sleep pods, gyms and other leisure facilities remain in some places of work, as we move forwards into the next decade of the twenty-first century, **workplace design will never fully return to that work and play concept of the 1990s.** Then, the office was treated almost as an extension of the home by introducing a domestic design language and the concept of wellbeing into the workplace.

Gone, too, is the ostentation and excess that characterized much design in the earlier part of the noughties, when expensive materials and gimmicky features became the norm of the office landscape, with scant regard for cost and long-term benefits. **Now it is no longer about how much you spend on an office fit-out, but how you spend it.**

Today's progressive office design is essentially concerned with effective resource management: a new responsibility for the modern architect. It includes managing all resources efficiently, from budgets to materials, as well as ideas. **Being ecologically aware and cost-efficient has become an integral part of good design.**

We have reached a state of effective pragmatism, where architects make sure every element of the modern office works as hard as the staff do. A reception area is not just a place to meet and greet guests, but provides a useful space for mobile workers. If directors are allocated a cellular office, this is used as another meeting room when vacant. And while hotdesking is an outmoded buzzword, the concept of **flexible working has evolved to meet the need for greater staff capacity in a decreasing floor plate.**

Considering the environment is no longer confined to token gestures, such as recycling bins or office plants. Developers, architects and end-users are more eco-conscious than ever before. While legislation has dictated this to some extent, it is every stakeholder's growing awareness of an office's carbon footprint that has really made environmentally sound measures a 'need to have' rather than a 'nice to have'.

Rainwater harvesting, biomass boilers, increased natural ventilation and natural light are becoming more commonplace, and **designers are working hard to source materials that have serious green credentials**. At the same time, developers realize the cost savings that come from a building that wastes fewer resources.

Total Office Design highlights fifty international projects chosen to demonstrate that a **contemporary cost-conscious and eco-aware approach to design need not** stifle creativity but can function as a design catalyst. The workplaces featured undoubtedly have the 'wow' factor now, but they also use materials and layouts that mean the interiors will be appealing in the future as well.

The book is divided into three distinct categories, which reflect the diversity of projects in terms of size and approach across a range of industries. The first section is made up of **small, low-cost offices**, up to 500 sq m (5,382 sq ft). These projects embody the spontaneity and make-do-and-mend approach that have flourished in other areas of contemporary culture, from pop-up retail outlets to the increased popularity of DIY and homecrafts. What these offices lack in budget, they more than make up for in creativity. **We may be living in austere times, but that doesn't mean we can't have fun where we work, and take a more craft-led approach.**

Paul Coudamy's work with IT firm Bearstech in Paris is a perfect example of the creativity found in these small offices. The project used wood scraps rescued from dumps and skips around the French capital to create a concave ceiling and a framework that define various interior spaces. The recycled wood gives the office a raw aesthetic, but also has a practical function as an acoustic buffer.

Keeping an open mind was crucial when it came to choosing materials for many of the featured projects. Alrik Koudenburg and Joost van Bleiswijk's design for the advertising agency Nothing in Amsterdam was intended to be temporary, so an extremely low-cost office was created from cardboard. 1,500 pieces were cut out and simply slotted together, making the office easy to transport elsewhere. Being both a recycled and recyclable material, cardboard ticked the environmentally friendly box too. The space is split into three zones: the reception area, the communal area and the workstations.

And to maximize the space, Koudenburg and Bleiswijk created an upper platform, supported by wooden beams, where the partners who run Nothing sit. The cardboard is sturdy enough to withstand around two years' wear and tear and its use reflects the aspirations of many start-ups to create strikingly innovative workplaces without significant capital outlay.

Staying in the Dutch capital for the moment, i29 interior architects have achieved a seamless look on a budget. In their design for Gummo their aim was to make an installation-like space that reflected the creative agency's personality; this was achieved through the use of a spray-painting treatment on reused furniture.

Below left: The designer Paul Coudamy used wood salvaged from Parisian skips to form a new internal structure for the Bearstech headquarters. **Below middle**: This desk, spray-painted with polyurea hotspray, is part of the furniture that defines advertising agency Gummo's office in Amsterdam. **Below right**: A demountable modular system of furniture, made from cardboard, forms the basis for the Nothing offices by Alrik Koudenburg and Joost van Bleiswijk.

Utilitarian elements can often be refashioned to become design focal points, as was the case in the offices of the non-profit organization TED, who promote new ideas in the fields of technology, entertainment and design. Here the standard steel parts of the ceiling, which distribute the services around the office, form the basis for the workplace colour scheme.

Back in Shoreditch, East London, the Klassnik Corporation used inexpensive materials such as birch-faced plywood and polished concrete. In keeping with the need for flexibility within these smaller spaces, the ground floor of this office contains modular storage units on castors; these can easily be reconfigured like a jigsaw, depending on what kind of space is required – be it a gallery, a library or even a retail space. At the heart of this scheme is a real desire to reconceive the most humble of pieces of office furniture to make this space multipurpose: filing cabinets are enveloped in a ribbon desk and a similarly bespoke approach was taken when it came to the meeting tables. The project responds to the creative staff's need for a place where they could develop ideas – something common to many of the smaller projects in the book.

Mid-range, commercial offices, 501–2,200 sq m (5,393–23,680 sq ft), often retain a more classical approach to interior design. They place some emphasis on green elements and are conceived on tight budgets. Architectural practice Rios Clementi Hale's own offices transformed an old building in Los Angeles, and reflect the trend for non-hierarchical, open-plan working. The project's exposed timber and ductwork is a familiar sight within contemporary workplaces.

Mid-range workplaces are also determined to be anything but mediocre. In an attempt **to rise above the competition they may go for an 'office as a local landmark' approach**, such as the Austrian motor technology firm Prisma Engineering. Architects SPLITTERWERK clad the manufacturing plant in graphic tiles to create a pixellated surface that dazzles from afar. Inside, the office space is kept clean-cut with exposed concrete floors counterbalanced by large, colourful artworks on the meeting room walls. In Milan, studiometrico converted a former cinema into the headquarters of skateboarding brand 'bastard'. Here a light, deft design touch was deployed – surfaces were simply painted black, and original features, such as a marble floor and concrete pillars, retained.

At Pullpo Creative Lab in Santiago, Chile, it was again important to work sympathetically with the industrial backdrop, in this case a former salt factory, but also to create a modern workplace suitable for a twenty-first-century creative agency. In order to balance the scale of the old building, architect Hania Stambuk created a series of flexible units for working, meeting and displaying campaigns, an approach that maintains a human scale in this medium-sized office.

At Langland's offices in Windsor

in the United Kingdom, Jump Studios have used a central spine of workspaces – library space, storage and break-out areas, tea points, and the reception – to break down barriers between teams. The spine is clad in white tiles and features green upholstery, providing a bright, visual connection well suited to the scale of the space, as well as conveying a sense of cleanliness and hygiene that underpins the branding of this healthcare advertising agency.

The final category is **large-scale commercial workplaces,** which are more than 2,200 sq m (23,680 sq ft). These offices are typically those of big, blue chip firms, which require significant square footage for their employees. Although these projects have larger budgets in total, money still has to be spent efficiently. The clients are keen to acquire official green accreditation or certification for their buildings, such as LEED (Leadership in Energy & Environmental Design) in the USA, or BREEAM (BRE Environmental Assessment Method) in Europe. To avoid 'silo working' – the reluctance of a large workforce to interact across departmental boundaries – **these offices encourage inter-departmental collaboration**, encouraged by the interior design of break-out spaces, corridors and even staircases.

At the University of Edinburgh, architects Bennetts Associates have used the scale of the Potterrow development, which houses the School of Informatics, to facilitate users'

interaction via dramatic 'wormhole' stairways. In London, the council headquarters for the Borough of Newham flies the flag for innovation in the public sector. Interior designers ID:SR have not only persuaded the client to move to more flexible desking solutions, but have also created a colourful, inspiring range of informal workspaces.

Large-scale projects can lead to a seismic shift in the way staff work. Microsoft's offices in Amsterdam are a shining example of the use of technology to optimize working procedures. No staff member has, or needs, a desk when each employee has a laptop and a mobile phone. Instead, staff are encouraged to work wherever they feel is most productive, whether that's a café area, work carousel or even a relaxation zone.

This book also looks at how successfully these larger projects have responded to their environments, from the home of the International Fund for Animal Welfare in an outstandingly beautiful part of Cape Cod to Vodafone's Portuguese base, skilfully integrated with Porto's iconic traditional architecture by Barbosa & Guimarães.

Especially in the current financial climate, large-scale office projects have to justify major new builds by adding value to the urban context and the immediate local environment. Unilever's new office in Hamburg has set the benchmark for the city's ongoing regeneration project HafenCity. Behnisch Architekten have, metaphorically and aesthetically,

created a ship that houses a spa, a restaurant and a shop, all of which are open to the public, with a terrace overlooking the harbour as a local focal point.

Rojkind's design for Nestlé's Latin American headquarters in Mexico is a prime example of how **creative workplace design can drive brand identity.** The clever twist of quoting the traditional architectural heritage of the region in a modern way is a visual expression of what this 'competence centre' does in terms of product innovation.

In short, *Total Office Design* is an invaluable and informative guide to workplace design in the new economy.

SMALL

(Up to 500 sq m)

Over the past decade, advertising agencies typically chose an office design that reflected their 'work and play' ethos: a multicoloured interior echoing the aesthetic of a kindergarten playroom. Today, however, that element of play has matured into the mantra 'reduce, reuse, recycle', as shown here by i29's design for advertising agency Gummo. Its monolithic grey fit-out stands in line with the agency's house-style colours but also ticks all the boxes regarding affordable and ecological qualities.

Given that Gummo plan to occupy the space for only two years, i29 came up with a design solution that would impact the environment and the client's wallet as little as possible by sourcing all of the required furniture second hand. Many items, from the desks to the pool table, including decorative objects such as a figure of Jesus Christ, were collected locally at markets and charity shops or bought in auctions on Marktplaats, the Dutch version of eBay. Furniture was also brought over from Gummo's previous office.

The trick was to get the interior to look and feel as good as new, despite reusing old furniture. Here, i29 were proactive and first cleaned then spray-painted every item with polyurea hotspray, a solvent-free and highly durable rubber coating. The coat covers almost any material, including wood, steel, fabrics and flooring. As a result, the space radiates a unified ambience rather than the jumbled mixture of disjointed objects that the initial collection of untreated items presented.

For i29, the inspiration came from rethinking the office fit-out as an installation of the company's personality. But the bottom line remains that the space has to function as a workplace. To guide staff through the office space, i29 painted grey squares onto the concrete floor. The shapes frame each area separately and delimit spaces such as the reception, working zone, the lounge, a mini grandstand for presentations and the canteen. The desks within this open-plan space are kept anonymous, as Gummo runs a 'clear desk' policy so that anyone can sit anywhere, simply connect their laptop and start working.

All in all, the office is a perfect example of austerity chic. The spray-paint treatment of reused furniture allows the workspace to expand or reduce very easily should the company grow, shrink or move – a prerequisite for the twenty-first-century creative office. Post-recession, this inspired yet simple approach, based on temporary occupancy and upgrading existing items, calls for more interpretations.

GUMMO OFFICE

Architect: **i29 interior architects**
Client: **Gummo**
Location: **Amsterdam, the Netherlands**
Completed: **February 2009**
Size: **450 sq m (4,840 sq ft)**
Budget: **€30,000**

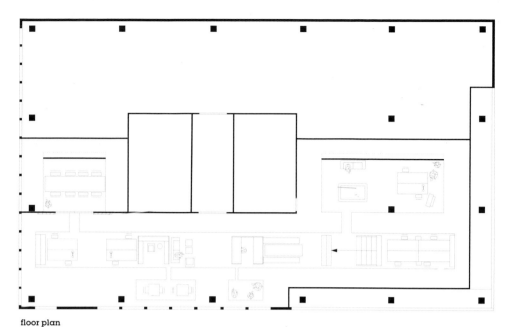

floor plan

Pages 12, 14–15: Salvaged furniture and items collected from flea markets have been treated with a rubber-based paint to integrate them with the office design; grey squares painted on the floor delineate different workspaces.

Opposite: An eclectic collection of vintage objects and used office furniture, such as sofas, dressers and desks, have been given new life and unified through the use of colour.

This page: Plans show the arrangement of the workstations, which are aligned in a single row like a central boulevard running through the office space.

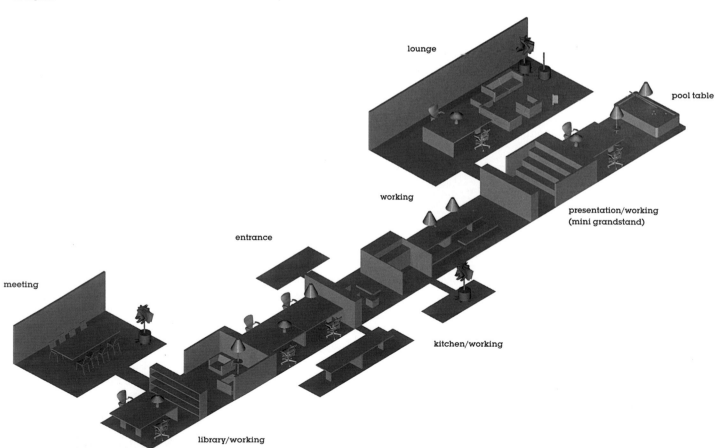

lounge

pool table

working

presentation/working
(mini grandstand)

entrance

meeting

kitchen/working

library/working

'Work autonomously but feel like part of a team' is a common ethos in agencies, and Syzygy, an international online marketing agency, wanted an office that communicated just that. The company hired eins:eins Architekten to design an office fit-out in the Gutruf Haus, a historic building in the centre of Hamburg. The project is based on a single piece of furniture – a sculptural desk formation makes Syzygy's workplace stand out among the other firms (a sister company and an architecture practice) on the newly refurbished floor.

The client liked the popular concept of everyone sitting at one communal desk, which is often found in creative agencies, most famously at Mother in London, designed by Clive Wilkinson. Eins:eins took this idea and tweaked it, getting everyone to sit 'inside' the same desk. Metaphorically the design suggests 'we're all in this together'.

The result is a sleek, pure surface with fourteen integrated working units. The single white plywood desktop measures 3.20 × 17.10 m and practically fills the long narrow room, flanked by generous window bays on either side. The white surface contrasts with the dark brown of the furniture's underside. Individual workstations are designated by a cut-out space for each employee, completed by shelves built into the unit. The budget was kept low by repeatedly cutting one shape out of the plywood to create the individual workstations. Using vast quantities of a single inexpensive raw material as the main building block helped considerably to keep the budget in check.

The acoustics of the space are regulated through integrated waste products that are hidden in the ceiling, which also saves money and materials as the noise-absorbing construction prevents the need for further partitions. The light fittings in the ceiling demonstrate a design-oriented approach. The amorphous textile has lights integrated in a flush, wavelike fashion, which accentuates the impression of sitting in one snug enveloping piece of furniture. The clean white design of the communal desk stands in sharp contrast to the traditional Gutruf Haus architecture, with its old-fashioned lifts and mosaic flooring on the ground floor.

On one side of the office three individual office cells are available to staff. Here the overall design is repeated, but it works less well than in the large communal space. The kitchen is a separate room that has been fitted out with a soft orange seating corner for brainstorming

SYZYGY OFFICE

Architect/Design: **eins:eins Architekten**
Client: **Syzygy**
Location: **Hamburg, Germany**
Completed: **November 2009**
Size: **368 sq m (3,961 sq ft)**
Budget: **undisclosed**

sessions. Additionally, a large conference table is used mainly for tele-conferencing with Syzygy's head office. A sliding wall with a pin-board surface facing the room can close off two desks at the back as a private space in case client-sensitive meetings need to take place. This wall also regulates access to the bathrooms on the other side.

All in all, the furniture design mirrors the client's way of working, and provides a small, low-cost fit-out with maximum impact.

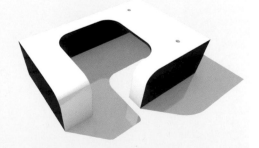

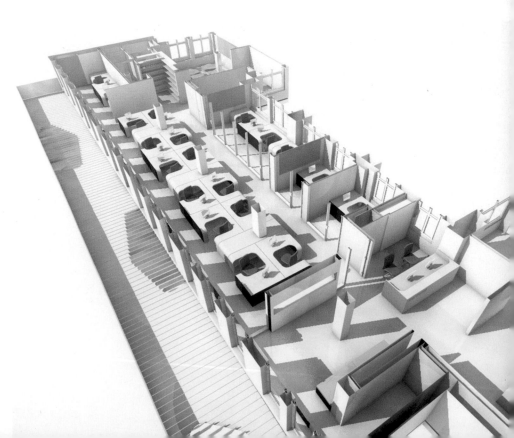

Page 18: A single continuous desk unit, incorporating individual bays, allows visual contact between team members and promotes a sense of connection, while providing a discrete space for each worker.

Above left: An aquarium adorns the wall between reception and the work floor.
Above right: The large conference table is often used for meetings with headquarters via tele-conferencing.
Right: The central desk unit encourages collaboration. There are enclosed meeting pods on one side of the unit and an outdoor terrace on the other.

Opposite: Staff can sit and work on the three surfaces that surround each chair, depending on whether they are working alone or sharing ideas with their colleagues.

In 2001, YCN launched as an annual award programme, highlighting recently graduated design talents in the UK. The company has since evolved into an agency that connects these young unknown designers with the big brands. So when YCN decided to move offices to 72 Rivington Street in Shoreditch, it took the obvious step of commissioning work from designers in its own ranks. The Klassnik Corporation, established by Tomas Klassnik, who gained architectural status working with FAT (Fashion Architecture Taste), was brought on board to develop the workplace design. His vision was then installed by Klassnik's former RCA student colleagues OKAY Studio, together with Rob Thuring. YCN's ethos of elevating young designers by profiling their work perfectly translated into an office fit-out commission, a choice that simultaneously kept the budget in check.

But it wasn't just about show-stopping design or cutting corners. Before the interior concept was born, the building needed structural work, such as levelling floors and rewiring electrics. When the time finally came to design the details, the designers' personal interest in identifying with the project's outcome helped to get the most 'bangs for bucks'. As recent graduates, Klassnik and OKAY (including Peter Marigold, Oscar Narud and Tomás Alonso) are trained in researching the most economic materials to bring their vision to life. Cheap resources include shuttering and birch-faced plywood, polished concrete and Perspex mirrors.

The workplace is divided into strata – three functions on three floors: a multipurpose space on the ground floor, acting as a shop front to the public; the administrative back office on the first floor; and the collaborative workspaces for meetings, focus group sessions and the kitchen on the second. In addition, YCN are developing the rooftop into a garden, which will include a greenhouse and space for staff to meet or have lunch, weather permitting. This clear-cut organization of working areas translates into a distinctive graphic visual of three floors and a rooftop, which YCN have now adopted as their brand logo; this simple stamp incorporates the office itself into the company's persona.

The bespoke storage/display solutions throughout the office show how the efficiency of multipurpose features can become part of an original design, and also helped to meet the low-budget brief. YCN's biggest problem in the old office was to organize the vast amounts of material submitted as competition entries. Klassnik arranged all storage alongside the walls, so as to allow the light to run uninterrupted through the space. To make use of all vertical surfaces, the storage units have whiteboard or blackboard surfaces facing the room. Staff can use them as noticeboards or easily reorder and organize things so they are instantly accessible.

Another efficient design feature is the ribbon desk on the admin floor. Klassnik designed a 'space within a space' by combining all of the desking into a continuous surface that varies in height and width throughout the floor. The design aids interaction among staff, and the various heights encourage impromptu meetings. At one point the ribbon loops into a door frame, creating a sense of connection between the entrance and the working environment. Our favourite design ingredient has to be Klassnik's method of 'framing ordinary objects'. For instance, conventional Bisley filing cabinets are enveloped into the ribbon desk unit at an unusual angle, sexing up the most standard of office furniture pieces.

The fit-out deliberately accentuates the charm of the original building, with its rickety brickwork, rather than masking it. Original hooks and pullies adorn the front, and the office interior stays true to the context of its location. Fortunately, this approach is more economical than replastering and the end result is original and unique – as much an extension of the YCN brand as a tribute to the designer talent involved.

YCN OFFICE

Architect: **The Klassnik Corporation**
Client: **YCN**
Location: **London, UK**
Completed: **April 2009**
Size: **210 sq m (2,260 sq ft)**
Budget: **c. £40,000**

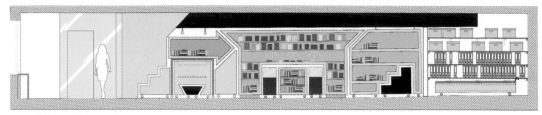

ground-floor section

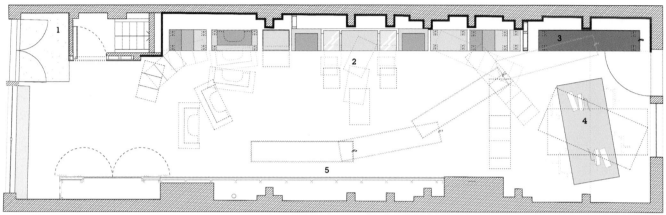

ground-floor plan

1 entrance
2 mobile display units start position
3 storage
4 workspace
5 gallery wall

Page 22: The exterior of YCN's office has kept its original East London look, and even retains its shop-front character – an added bonus.

Above: The ground-floor space can be transformed from event space to library or gallery, simply by moving the custom-made furniture units. **Left above**: Modular storage units fit together like pieces in a jigsaw puzzle, and can be tucked away into the wall when they do not need to be accessed regularly. **Left below**: The units are rolled out and configured to create an exhibition space.

Opposite: A mixture of units in edgy shapes can be fitted together in different ways and are on castors so they can easily be moved and rearranged (*left and right columns*). The YCN office doubles up as a library and a bookshop (*central column*).

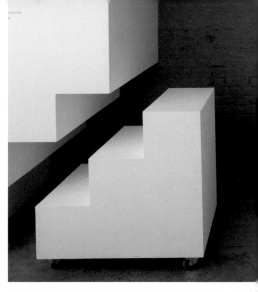

YCN.72 RIVINGTON STREET

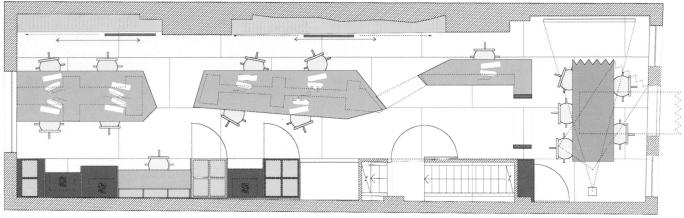

first-floor plan

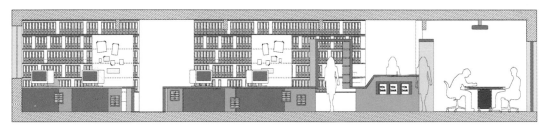

first-floor section

Page 26: The ribbon desk, designed by the Klassnik Corporation and produced by OKAY Studio, is made of affordable plywood; its strong, angular contours create a feeling of motion and continuity as it marches across the office floor.

Page 27: Plans show how the separate desk units, with storage on one side, are tied together by the ribbon design (*top*). The ribbon feature rears up to form a doorway arch in the middle of the room, which creates a sense of transition between different zones of the office space (*below left*). The wall can be used as a pin-board so that the team can share and develop ideas (*below right*).

This page: In response to YCN's brief to create more storage for all the materials they are sent, Klassnik came up with a variety of storage solutions. In addition to the three floors, Klassnik converted the rooftop into an outdoor break-out area.

Opposite: The bespoke-designed conference table cantilevers out of the building, advertising the office to the street.

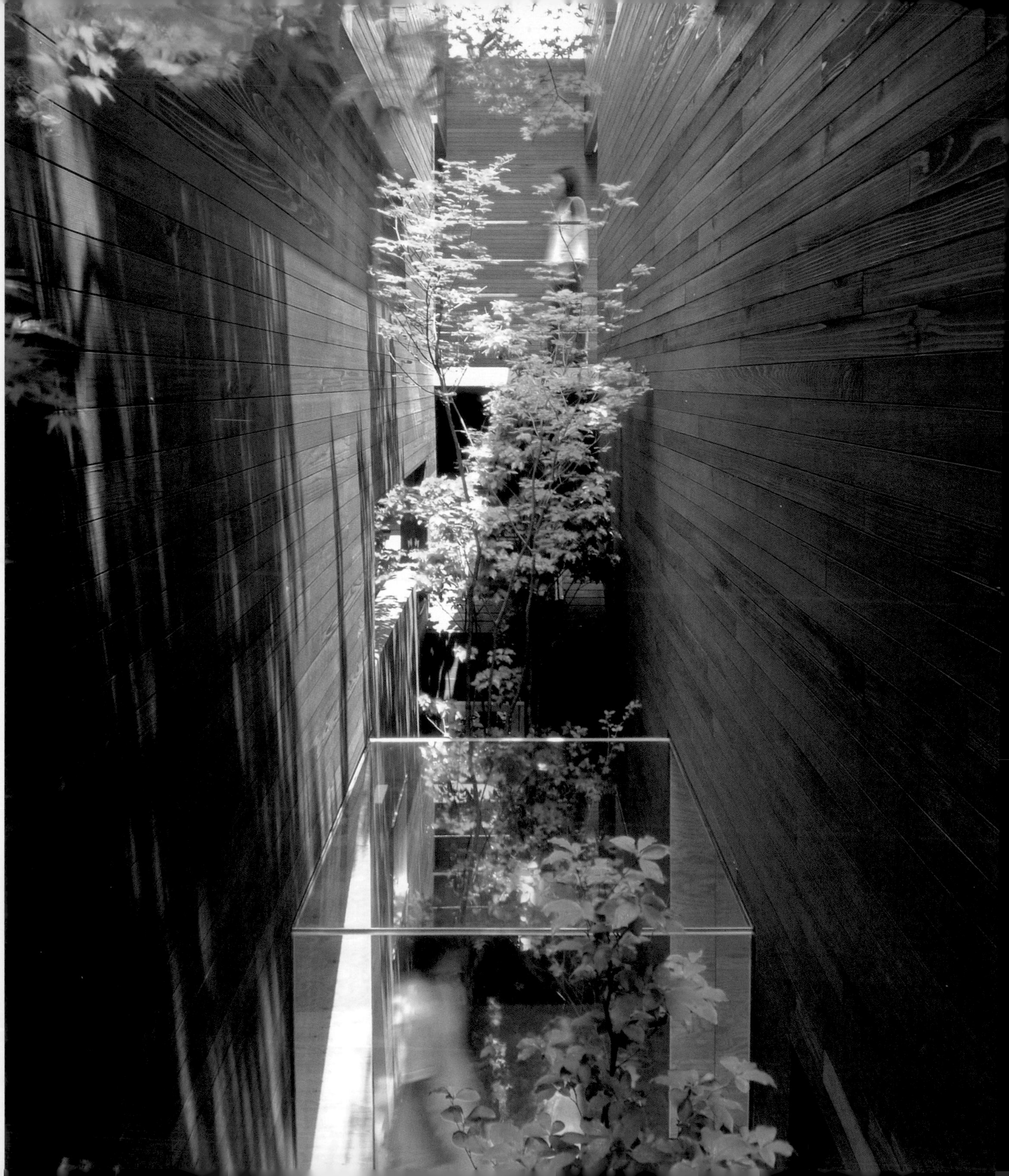

Multi-tenant office buildings worldwide are notorious for prioritizing profits through maximum use of floor space. That is, of course, in the interest of the clients (the property developers), who are thinking of their rental income. As a result, few buildings manage to provide all of the offices' tenants with equal shares of light and space. Keisuke Maeda at UID Architects took on the challenge of breaking with the 'superficial architecture' of multi-tenant offices and has developed a new model based on democratic space management.

The key concept for the MORI x Hako office build in the Hiroshima prefecture is to ensure equal portions of light and inspiring views for all three sub-offices. Direct feedback from the tenants confirmed the contemporary workplace mantra that daylight and natural settings – greenery, views, water features – are integral elements for creating a humane and, consequently, a productive office environment. The main challenge here is that the construction site is a narrow (10 m) yet deep (50 m) plot in a residential area. To give access to daylight to all of the offices, and not just the one at the front of the building, UID applied an original 'layering technique'. They broke down the site into boxes that are stacked so as to make use of every wall as a horizontal and vertical connector, dividing the space, respectively, between front and back, and between floors.

In the middle of the building, the central 'box' houses the staircase. In this box, trees were planted to create a 'forest'. The three offices surround the central space, and every wall has large, generous windows, which the architects refer to as 'openings'; these seem to be randomly positioned but their arrangement is calculated to ensure that maximum daylight is available to the work floors. The windows also frame the best views of the outside world and the trees in the atrium. The visibility between the offices mimics nature's organic configurations: from each office you can see the other spaces, yet the forest prevents a clear view, ensuring privacy for each tenant.

In effect, UID thought of each office 'box' as a stand-alone building, treating the inner connecting walls like exterior walls by giving them windows. The prevailing interior material is Japanese cedar wood. It enhances the natural atmosphere of the space and fits into the local context. This traditional Japanese wood has proven to be very durable, making it a sustainable feature in the long-run. In addition, the cedar is very economical. UID used all-purpose battens, which are usually applied as a finish on exterior walls, for both the outer walls and various interior parts including joints, internal setbacks and wall layers. By ordering only one material in high quantities the price point was kept relatively low.

The furniture inside is sleek, and the large flowing desk surfaces extend the general democratic approach of the design to the micro level of each workspace. Ultimately, the flow of the design encourages a natural movement of people throughout the space, a common prerequisite for today's good office design. And MORI x Hako's example shows that these principles can also be integrated into multi-tenant offices.

MORI X HAKO OFFICES

Architect: **UID Architects**
Client: **MORI x Hako**
Location: **Fukuyama, Japan**
Completed: **January 2009**
Size: **360 sq m (3,870 sq ft)**
Budget: **€675,000**

Page 30: Feedback from tenants showed that greenery and natural settings were thought to be key to a productive working environment. UID took this into account in introducing live trees into the central atrium.

Above left: From each office a corridor leads out into the central garden. **Above right**: The inside walls, with irregularly disposed windows, create the impression of exterior walls facing onto a street, and give a pleasing sense of ambiguity to the thoroughfares in the building. **Right**: The Japanese timber cladding on the walls contrasts in colour and texture with the smooth concrete steps.

Opposite: The custom-carved desktop accommodates individual workstations and even incorporates live trees into the working environment.

Left: The design concept, which resolves the building into a series of stacked boxes, is followed through in the emphatic treatment of windows and doorways as stark square openings.

Below: The space is organized to integrate the indoor garden with the different offices. **Bottom**: The minimalist interior uses squares and plants as the main design features.

1 approach
2 salon
3 workspace
4 consulting room
5 meeting room

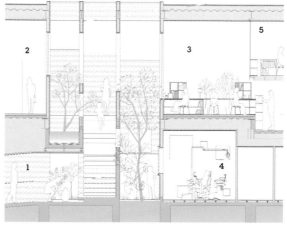

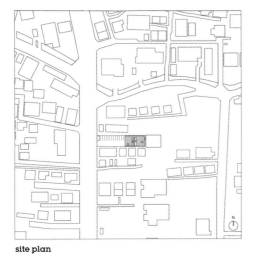

site plan

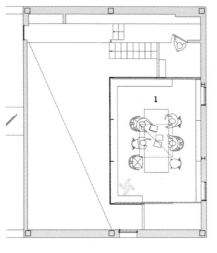

This page: The multi-tenant building includes clinic rooms (*bottom left*), as well as office space (*centre left*). Each floor has a different layout but the central garden strongly integrates the entire design.

Opposite: Natural daylight enters the central court through a large opening in the roof, contrasting with softer lighting set into and against the warm wood of the ceilings and walls.

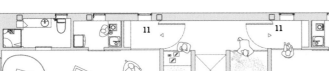

second floor

1 meeting room
2 counselling room
3 waiting area
4 workspace
5 reception
6 doctor's room
7 consulting room
8 disinfecting room
9 x-ray room
10 staff room
11 entrance

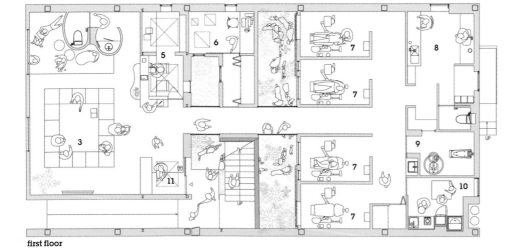

first floor

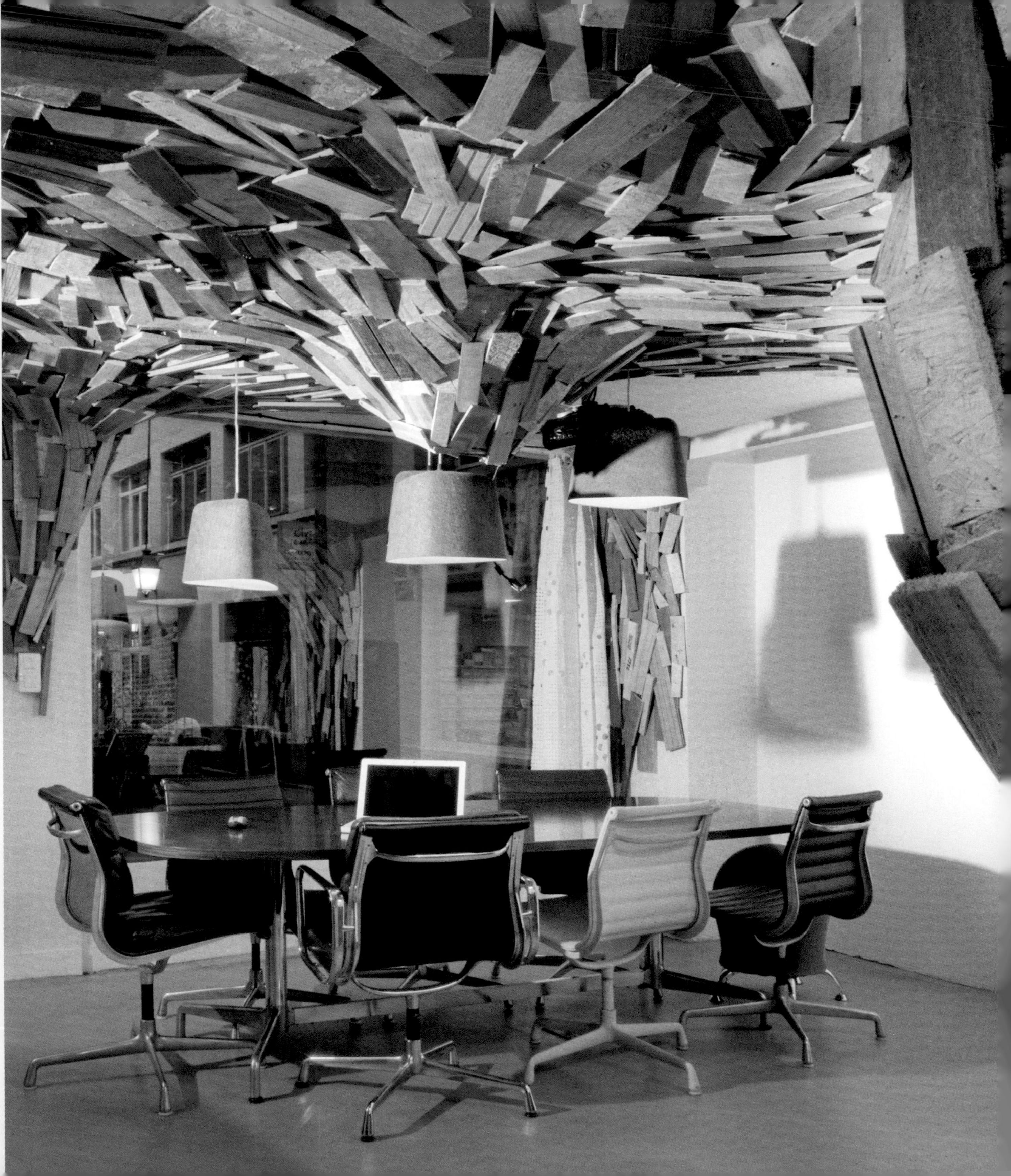

Tucked away in a Paris alley lies Bearstech's new headquarters. The computer company took over an old retail space, and called on Paul Coudamy to transform it into a workplace. The brief was to design an office that reflects the company's innovative and 'wild' approach to virtual technology. Coudamy took inspiration from the name, and possibly from the common perception of IT people hiding in dark chambers, and set out to create a 'bear cave'. The small space already had an intimate feel about it, and Coudamy's use of wood scraps to craft a concave ceiling creates a captivating cavernous atmosphere.

The floor plan is broken down into the usual office trilogy of work, leisure and meeting spaces. Yet all parallels to typical workplaces end here. The walls and ceiling are covered in a colourful mix of 100% reclaimed wood pieces rescued from dumps and skips around Paris. All 2,500 wood pieces have their own history, a random collection of old bourgeois floorboards, abandoned palettes, shipping crates, furniture samples, and planks with marks and scratches to emphasize the genuine rawness of the material (and its source).

Needless to say the accumulation of waste wood was free, an ideal case of resourceful economics, not to mention the sustainable benefit of giving a second lease of life to existing waste materials. It is not news that reusing old wood is more eco-friendly than using recycled materials that have gone through a production chain. Yet the contemporary factor here is the way 'rubbish' is applied without being retouched to create an attractive, coherent and original workplace.

Coudamy insists that the need to be cost-effective stimulated the design scheme. He first built a primary wood framework, not dissimilar to one on a construction site, and then nailed the individual wood scraps piece by piece onto it, starting from the floor up to the central point above the main meeting table. The idea was to create a vortex, based on associations of chaotic mass in the cyber world, which he found evoked aerial pictures of post-Tsunami rubble. Inspired by these images, Coudamy designed an organic, and in a way anarchical, space for the client.

All the electrics, such as plugs, video devices and projectors, are integrated into this central spine and the wires are hidden inside the structure, yet still easy to access. The shelves and a custom-made bench that separates the workstations from the meeting room are made of recycled

BEARSTECH HEADQUARTERS

Architect/Design: **Paul Coudamy**
Client: **Bearstech**
Location: **Paris, France**
Completed: **May 2009**
Size: **60 sq m (650 sq ft)**
Budget: **undisclosed**

honeycomb cardboard and covered in natural felt. The ecological footprint is extremely low, as the cardboard is made from 70% recycled paper and is 100% recyclable. In addition to its intriguing look, the wooden cave structure provides an excellent acoustic setting, especially good for noise control during meetings.

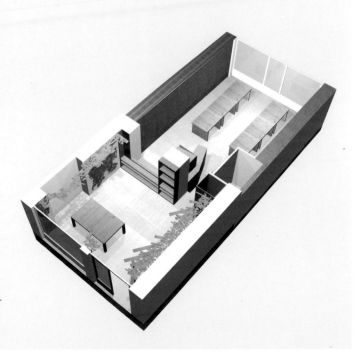

Pages 38 and 39: The wood for the 'cave' was salvaged from Paris skips. The structure provides an acoustic baffle to the office space, particularly useful in the meeting areas.

This page: The use of reclaimed wood continues throughout the office; it gives the interior an organic feel.

Opposite: The technical facilities necessary in a modern workplace are integrated into the spine of the structure, creating a seamless and somewhat informal aesthetic in this unique office.

This modest yet elegant office for a boutique art and graphic studio in downtown Toronto called for a clear, thoughtful design using a reduced palette of inexpensive materials to meet the client's tight budget. The project also had a very tight timescale. The office is situated on the top floor of a historic warehouse, with limited access to natural light because it is surrounded on three sides by other buildings. Numerous slot windows were created in outer walls so that light could enter the interior. The space was stripped down to its essential elements, such as the original beams and columns, which were then celebrated rather than being reinvented or covered up. Ceiling joists and existing ductwork were also exposed.

Efforts were taken to make this an appropriate backdrop for what is a creative company. Hambly and Woolley use a lot of colour in their projects and presentations, which the designers found inspiring and did not want to compete with – hence the neutral colour scheme throughout the space. The dominant colours are neutral, and the designers colour-coded the workspaces to match the colours of the client's logo. The client wanted its staff of designers to have private workspaces so the Cindy Rendely team created separate offices with closed doors. The offices around the perimeter are punctuated with frosted glazing, allowing more daylight into the heart of the floor, while at the same time creating visual openness. Employees also need space to collaborate and to lay out their designs for review, so there is an area of large tables for this purpose.

Inexpensive materials were used in the project. Throughout the space, minimal yet sophisticated patchwork wood millwork was used, with laminate and reclaimed wood making up the other main materials. In a way, the materials did not matter as the attention of both users and visitors to the offices is focused on the proportions and details of the scheme. Boundaries between plinths, edges, walls and furniture seem to blur, giving something of a sculptural quality to the workspace. In addition, the newly introduced wood surfaces complement existing wooden floors and ceilings. All of the doors are simple wood planks with a matt lacquer finish, in keeping with the intended raw appearance. The end result has a warm and casual aesthetic.

HAMBLY AND WOOLLEY STUDIO

Architect: **Cindy Rendely Architexture**
Client: **Hambly and Woolley**
Location: **Toronto, Canada**
Completed: **2007**
Size: **370 sq m (3,980 sq ft)**
Budget: **CAN $95,000**

Opposite: The architects wanted to keep a fairly neutral colour scheme within the space and so used a reduced palette of colours, and also stripped down original features such as the beams.

Page 44: The interior acts as a blank canvas for the client's creative ideas and colourful presentations (*top left*). To give warmth and texture to the project, timber was chosen as the main material (*top right*). The offices are located around the outside of the floor plate, and the perimeter walls are punctuated with glazing to allow more daylight into the individual rooms (*bottom*).

Page 45: The architects have created an almost seamless quality to the walls, floors and furnishings, mainly through the use of different types of wood (*bottom left*). Sufficient artificial lighting was a key requirement, as natural daylight was limited.

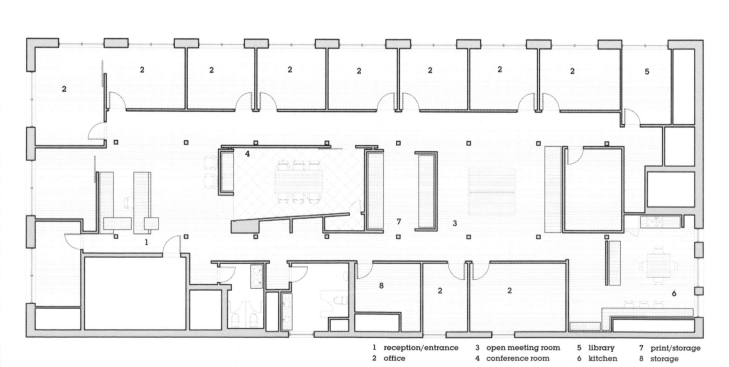

1 reception/entrance   3 open meeting room   5 library   7 print/storage
2 office   4 conference room   6 kitchen   8 storage

To design an office on a shoestring might curb some architects' enthusiasm, but for Alrik Koudenburg it became a 'dream' project. The creative services agency Nothing was looking for a temporary office fit-out, ideally a demountable modular system that would last them two years, though they only had a limited budget to play with. So it was either an ordinary Ikea office that no one would talk about or a cheap installation everyone would want to see. Obviously the latter was more tempting, but to achieve this they were in need of a designer with an artistic touch. They came across Alrik Koudenburg, a Dutch concept designer, who had art-directed original campaigns for Nike and Heineken. In return for the low fee, Nothing gave Koudenburg free reign over the design concept. With that, the office became the designer's fantasy portfolio piece.

Taking the agency's name and philosophy as a starting point (Nothing – to make something from nothing), Koudenburg developed a vision of a model world on paper. He started designing the volumes and functions of the space with elaborate drawings and sketches. The perfect solution came to him when he saw Michel Gondry's film *The Science of Sleep* and immediately fell for the scene where a dream sequence is set in a cardboard construction. On researching the material he found a low-priced supplier in Italy who was prepared to sell at production cost: 500,000 sq m of industrial cardboard for €3,500.

Industrial cardboard ticked all the boxes: it costs 'next to nothing' and at 15 mm depth, with a reinforced honeycomb structure, Koudenburg could guarantee it would last for a minimum of two years. It tells the Nothing story perfectly. Koudenburg collaborated with a former colleague from the Design Academy Eindhoven, Joost van Bleiswijk. Together they constructed an office using van Bleiswijk's 'no screws, no glue' method to assemble the cardboard structure. Van Bleiswijk involved his team of student CAD draughtsmen at the academy in designing the intricate details. This resulted in 1,500 separate cardboard pieces cut via a computer-assisted system and then simply slotted together to strengthen the construction. The method adds a further ecological advantage to the use of a recycled and recyclable material as no additional glue or supporting elements are required, therefore minimizing the use of chemicals and preventing waste when the furniture is dismantled. All other features, such as the tube lighting and wires, are hidden under the structure. MDF was used for the floor, as it visually resembles cardboard.

NOTHING OFFICE

Design: **Alrik Koudenburg + Joost van Bleiswijk**
Client: **Nothing**
Location: **Amsterdam, the Netherlands**
Completed: **March 2009**
Size: **100 sq m (1,080 sq ft)**
Budget: **€30,000**

The office has three zones: a public area (reception), a communal area and the workstations. The agency's two partners sit on an upper floor, above the kitchen and storage area, from where they have a view of the entire space. The upper platform and the stairs are supported by wooden beams, but apart from that the whole structure is freestanding; it sits like a 'fortress' in an otherwise untouched standard white room within a multi-occupancy office building. You can walk around or underneath the cardboard structure or even climb on top of it.

Naturally, the material has a shelf-life, but all the surfaces are varnished and therefore 'coffee-spill-proof'. And at that price (100 sq m of industrial cardboard for 70 euro cents), an additional desk or replacement for a damaged surface certainly does not constitute a problem, even on such a tight budget. The cardboard walls function as a blank canvas, encouraging staff to draw on them. But what makes the space stand out, even among other cardboard designs, is the contrast between the cheap, waste material and its art deco-style ornamentation. The design is all about giving an industrial material a luxury feel.

Page 46: The innovative use of cardboard throughout the office defines this temporary fit-out: even the company logo has been carved in cardboard.

Opposite: The detail and solid design of the cardboard structure give a cheap, temporary material a sturdy quality.

Above: A U-shaped sofa in the executive's office creates a congenial meeting space (*left*). Extra workstations have been added to the side of the main structure (*right*). **Below**: A digital graphic shows the whole cardboard installation.

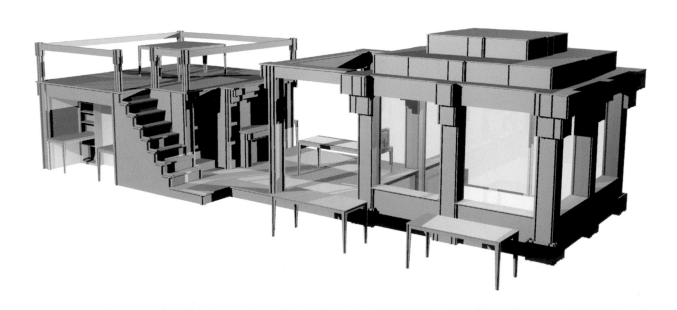

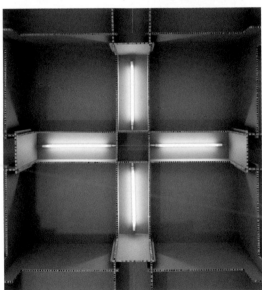

This page: From the graphics on the walls to the clean-cut furniture, cardboard has never looked so good. And the original thinking that went into the design is as evident in the details as in the overall concept.

Opposite: A room within a room: the cardboard girders create a sense of separate areas, even though the structure is built in one room.

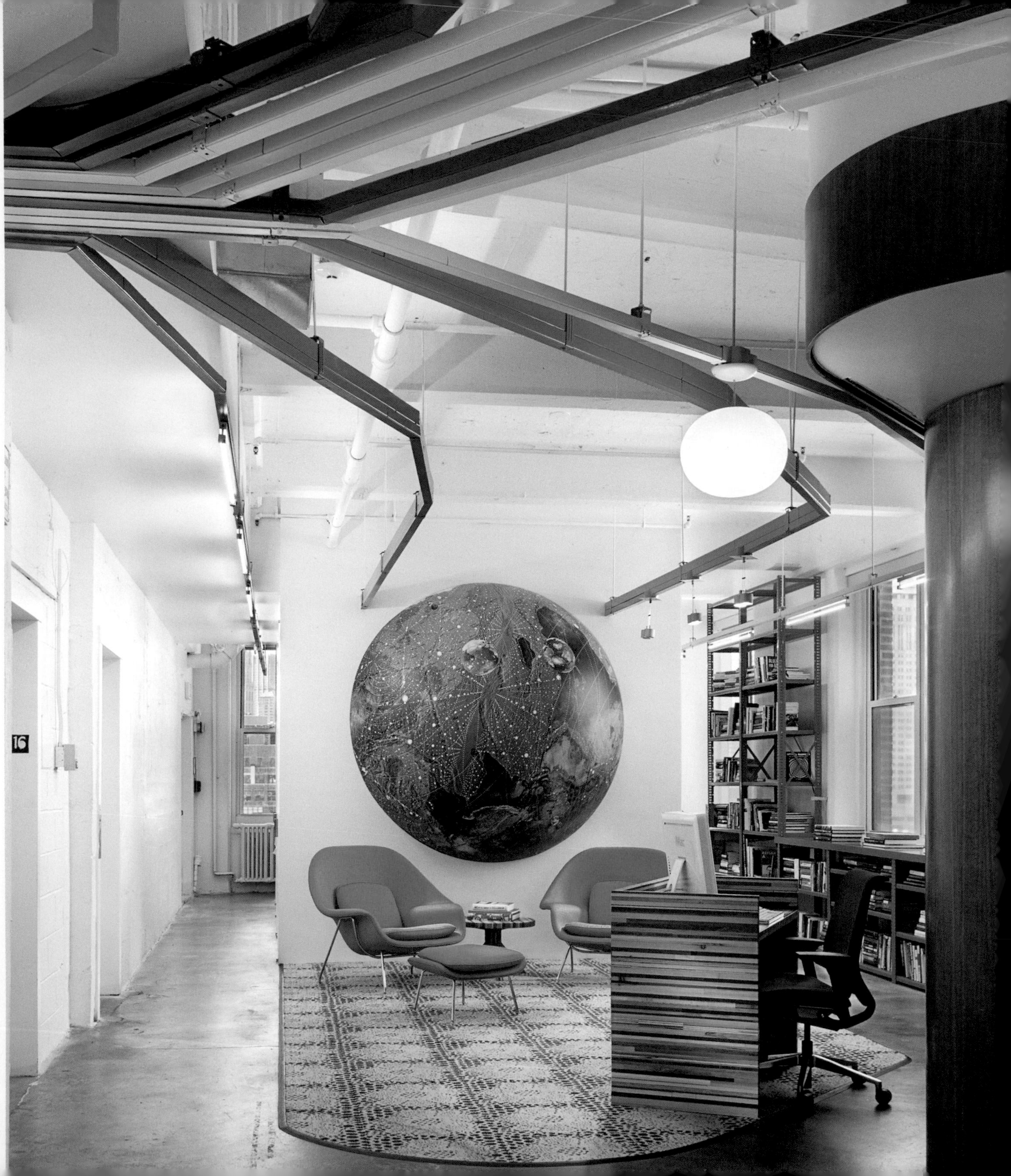

TED Office/Tina Manis

The mission of global non-profit organization TED (Technology, Entertainment, Design) is to disseminate 'ideas worth spreading' through its annual conferences. As such the brief for its offices in Manhattan was to create a place where communication could flow continuously.

As a result, there are none of the usual rows and cubicles of the traditional US workplace. Instead the workspace is open, with multiple meeting areas.

Services that distribute data, media, lighting and communication usually impose certain restrictions on an office environment in terms of layout. To get around the problem in this particular workplace, the systems have been elevated to steel channels suspended from the ceiling.

As TED is a non-profit organization, keeping the budget under control was essential in leading the innovation of this workplace. The ceiling distribution system uses standard steel parts and takes advantage of a free system ceiling, as opposed to a more expensive raised-floor system. This allows for distribution of communications services (telephone wires, computer cabling, etc.) and lighting, as well as making upgrades straightforward as and when these are necessary.

This use of the ceiling plane enables the floor plate to be more open, to accommodate different types of work areas. The colours found on the steel channel system are echoed below in the various areas of the office, creating a spatial identity for TED in a range of vivid shades such as orange, turquoise and green, which are accented on walls and in the furniture.

In this workspace, a conference room grows organically out of a windowed corner. Its orientation allows it to be included in the open office, while a sliding wall can close off the space for larger private meetings.

Smaller meetings take place around the perimeter of the office, in corners and between the workstation spines. Editing suites and phone booths, with their contemporary red-buttoned walls, are more isolated from the main space for better acoustic control and greater confidentiality.

The space facilitates the notion of 'group and regroup'. It includes multiple meeting areas at different scales to foster easy exchanges between all the teams.

The design incorporates materials that fit the budget and were innovative solutions from local firms, such as Scrapile furniture made of repurposed scrap wood from New York factories. Other eco-materials include Flor modular carpet tiles, manufactured with recycled

TED OFFICE

Architect/Design: **Tina Manis Associates**
Client: **TED Conferences**
Location: **New York, USA**
Completed: **June 2008**
Floor space: **310 sq m (3,300 sq ft)**
Budget: **US $500,000**

content through carbon-neutral factories, and cradle-to-cradle elements from Steelcase modular workstations.

The overall aesthetic has a raw, industrial feel, into which colour has been injected to create an inspiring and professional place to work.

floor plan

1 reception
2 video
3 lounge
4 conference room
5 open office
6 small conference room
7 small meeting room
8 bathroom
9 electrical
10 storage

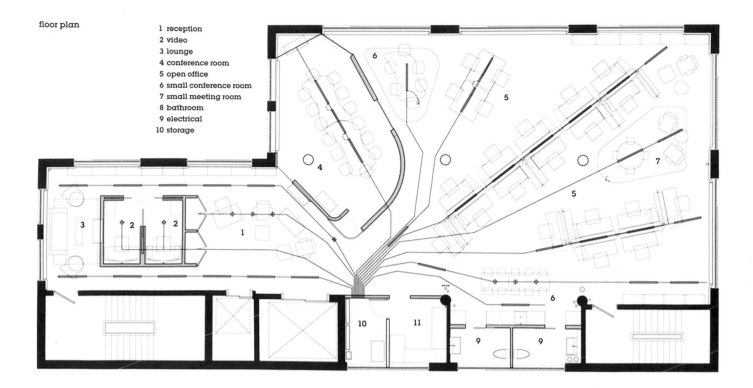

Page 52: The office avoids too corporate a look, creating a cosier informality through the warm textures of carpeting and upholstered seating.

Opposite: The core colour palette includes a vibrant orange, featured in the reception.

This page: The floor plan highlights the flow of the ceiling-mounted communications distribution system and the open office space.

Page 56: The vivid colour palette continues throughout the building: the bathroom uses a bright, modern shade of turquoise (*top left*); red is used in the TED office manifestations (transfers on glass panels) and brand identifiers (*top right*); and rich crimson phone booths with buttoned walls add a fun touch to the space, and give staff a place to hold confidential conversations (*bottom left*). A meeting space away from the open-plan environment also offers the opportunity for more private discussions (*bottom right*).

Page 57: Yellow accents on the seating provide colourful highlights in the kitchen area.

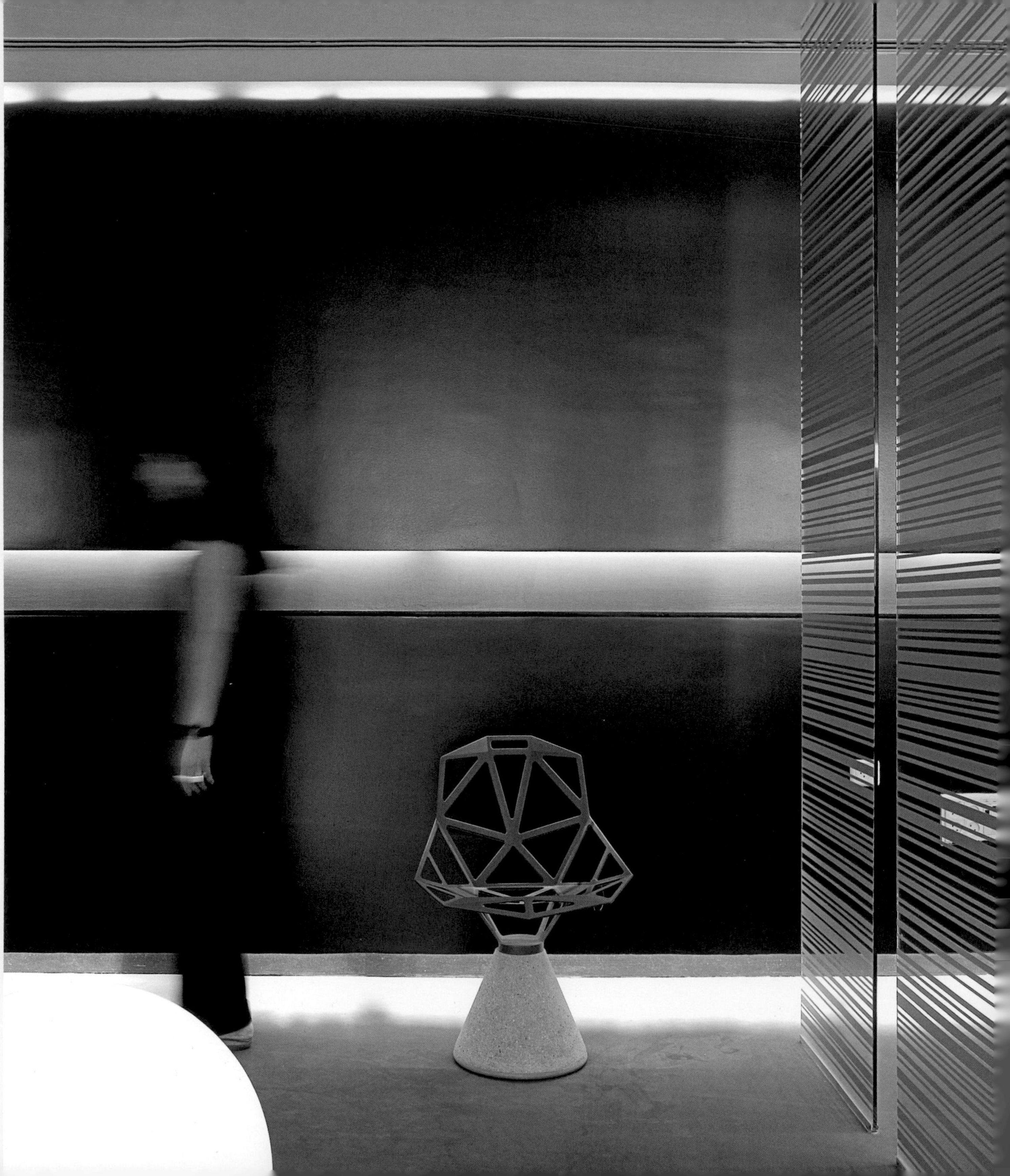

In today's climate, businesses linked to the financial sector are faced with a balancing act when it comes to redesigning their offices. Companies do not want to be seen to be wasting money on opulent designs in times when the repercussions of the worldwide economic crisis are still being strongly felt. Yet it is, now more than ever, vital that the workplace communicates a sense of solidity and reliability to clients and staff alike. For the finance industry the workplace is once again becoming synonymous with image.

The Israel office of financial services firm Global Factoring needed a refurbishment, and this was the ideal opportunity to portray the company's ethos in its environment: the brief to Tel Aviv-based architects Axelrod was to create a space that would convey strength in a subtle way. In response to that brief, Axelrod built a clean and focused environment, one that would be sensitive to the pressures of the business. Many features of the office, such as the dark wood and austere furniture, echo the past style of this conservative sector. The result is a modernist interpretation of the traditional financial space: here the wooden walls communicate solidity, the clean lines of the lights and the sleek furniture consistency. The furniture is lightweight, the masculinity commonly associated with the chosen colours is softened by the light slots that break up the spaces; the indirect lighting warms the atmosphere, giving the office a relaxed feel.

The architectural expression and attention to detail echo the precision so vital in the client's business transactions. Clean cuts, straight lines and solid surfaces dominate throughout. Axelrod used customized light fixtures to create niches and alcoves that help subtly to define the boundaries between private and public spaces. Walls appear elevated because of a backlit strip located at the bottom of the wall, bringing lightness to the mood and relieving pressure. Glass partitions, decorated with purpose-designed graphics, create physical separation yet maintain visual connections within the workspace and open up the floor. Furniture is deliberately unobtrusive – low sideboards and few chairs – to complement new ideas around transparency in the financial sector.

The architects' aim was to create a modernist aesthetic. The sealed concrete floor, glass walls, and minimalist furnishing and lighting still say 'banking', but the efficient reuse of the pre-existing shell demonstrates an economic design. Axelrod admit that by painting the walls remaining from the existing structure and using inexpensive wall decals (transfers), a cheap yet effective upgrade was achieved. They also focused on maximizing the use of natural light by partitioning the space with glass, and adopted energy-efficient lighting inside light slots, which have the incidental advantage of bringing strong linear accents to the room.

GLOBAL FACTORING OFFICE

Architect: **Axelrod Architects**
Client: **Global Factoring**
Location: **Herzliya, Israel**
Completed: **July 2007**
Size: **250 sq m (2,690 sq ft)**
Budget: **undisclosed**

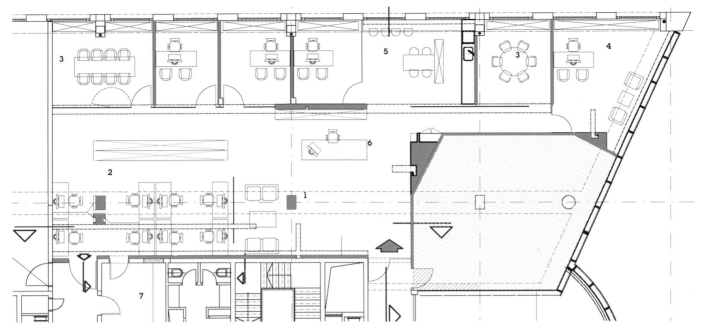

floor plan

1 lobby
2 trading floor
3 conference room
4 executive room
5 kitchen
6 reception
7 archive

Page 58: The linearity of the design is key to a visual representation of solid financial reliability: the brief was to create a space that subtly conveyed a feeling of strength.

Opposite: The recurring light features create tracks to guide workers and visitors alike through the space.

Above: The floor plan shows a conventional office layout, with open-plan space in the middle and a series of meeting rooms along one side. **Right**: Simple tables provide extra desk space to accommodate occasional workers.

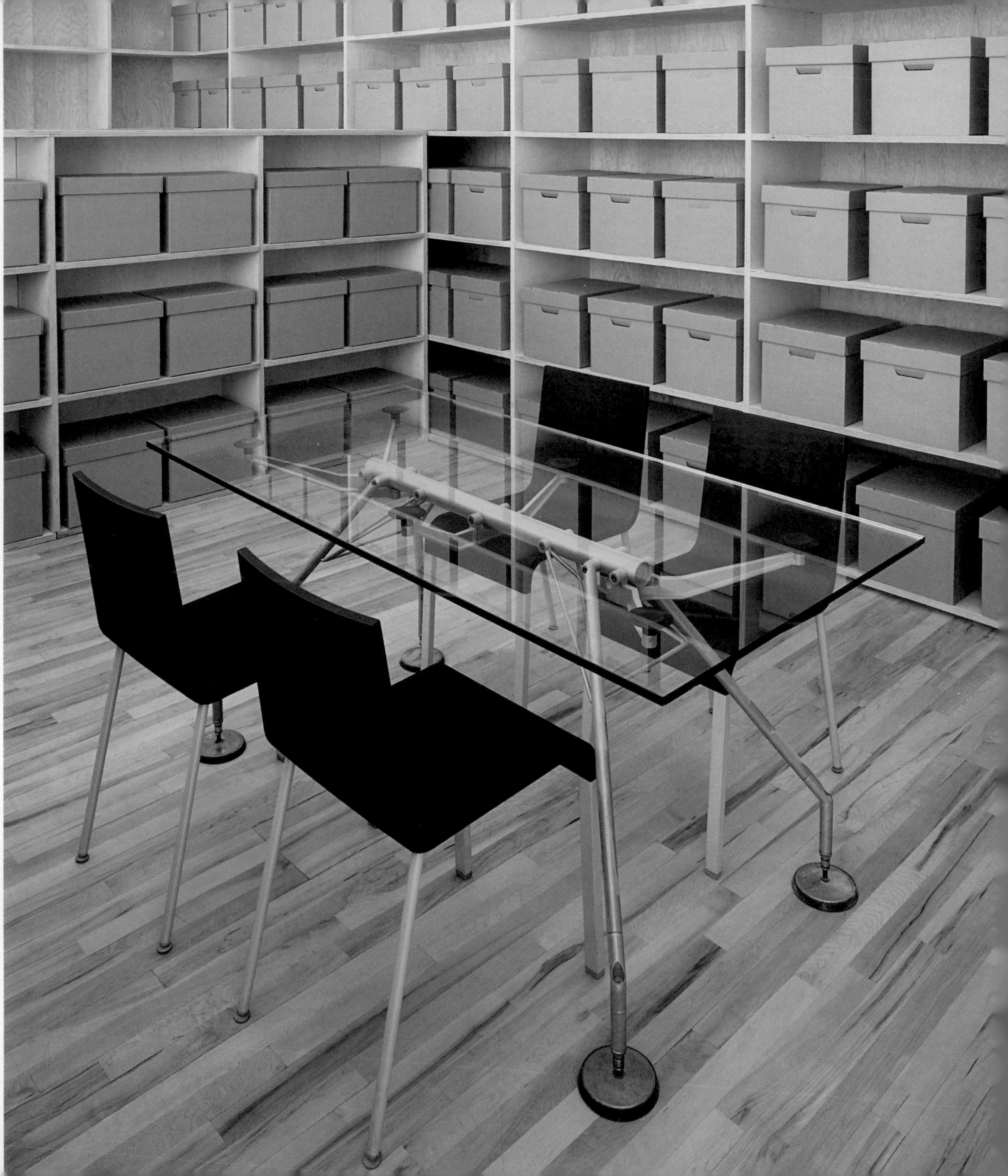

Design studio Carmody Groarke has produced a light-footed intervention into an old warehouse in Tooley Street, south London, in order to provide offices for non-profit agency The Architecture Foundation. The low-cost design functions not only as a workplace, but also as an exhibition space intended to promote new talent and ideas within contemporary architecture, urbanism and culture.

The no-nonsense design utilizes simple, robust materials – predominantly plywood. The blueprint for the design was rooted in what Carmody Groarke had done with their own workspace in Denmark Street, London, where even the marks and notes on the pieces of wood had been retained for authenticity. Essentially, the architects' approach is uncomplicated and honest, and does without designer furniture or expensive materials. Cost-wise, the project was about keeping expenses to a minimum, though the aim was nonetheless to produce a good-quality, functional fit-out.

The existing birds-eye maple floor of the Tooley Street warehouse was kept, and sustainably sourced Douglas fir was used on the walls. The furniture was constructed from birch-faced plywood, a material that will become lighter in the sunlight and so add character to the project as it ages. Bespoke storage, also made from plywood, was created for the dozen or so employees who sit in the open-plan environment. The wood was chosen for its warmth as well as its low price, and is complemented by white plaster on the ceiling and parts of the walls. Both materials work with the existing architectural features of the Edwardian building, such as the industrial pillars. In transforming the previous incarnation of the space, the architect had a blank canvas, except for the requirement to include a small kitchen, two bathrooms and an additional storage room.

The design for the exhibition space had to be flexible enough to accommodate The Architecture Foundation's diverse programme of events. Here, the cladding may look like a temporary installation, marked with holes and other damage caused by putting up exhibits, but it is in fact permanent, the wear and tear being part of the long-term workplace aesthetic. In this area there is also a new service bar. The sense of the temporary is echoed in the absence of a formal reception and names for the meeting rooms. Visitors enter the ground floor from the street, where the former shop front provides a window into the gallery space. The back office needed a visual connection to the exhibition space at the front of the

building: this was achieved through a simple grid pattern of fluorescent lighting, which provides an element of continuity throughout the space.

THE ARCHITECTURE FOUNDATION OFFICE

Architect: **Carmody Groarke**
Client: **The Architecture Foundation**
Location: **London, UK**
Completed: **May 2009**
Size: **167 sq m (1,800 sq ft)**
Budget: **undisclosed**

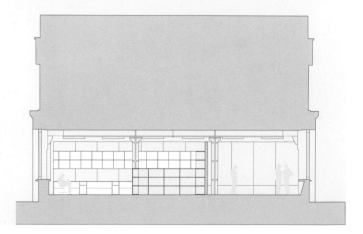

Page 62: Bespoke shelving adds to the practicality of this fit-out, but structural intervention was light and minimal, and many original features have been retained.

Page 63: The office is located on the ground floor of the building and features an open space, shown here on the right, facing onto the street.

This page: The simply laid-out space is designed to be multifunctional: as well as an office, it has an area for exhibitions and events.

Opposite: The use of plywood is central to the cost-effectiveness of the redesign for this Edwardian building.

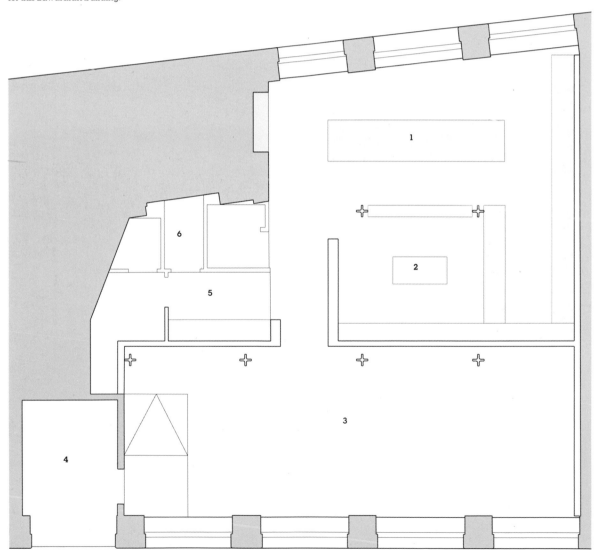

1 office
2 meeting room
3 project space
4 entrance foyer
5 kitchen
6 bathroom

floor plan

Office fit-outs for advertising agencies are notoriously 'wacky', and critics have long supposed this to be an attempt to impress clients looking for creative solutions. Yet Dutch agency KesselsKramer's London outlet exemplifies an unconventional workplace that is driven by economics, showing how efficiency and eccentricity can be perfect partners.

In terms of look and feel, KK's Hoxton space was meant to emulate the style of their Dutch base. Yet FAT's eclectic design concept focuses on maximizing the function of the given space by creating a 'hybrid office'. To prevent the space from being a homogenous interior, they took the radical decision to split it into two halves with a diagonal plywood wall. One half remains open as a gallery for KK events and exhibitions; the other half houses a row of individual rooms that each set an unexpected scene.

Inspired by KK's own work method of reappropriating the everyday, these workrooms show regular interior furnishings mixed in an unorthodox way. For instance, there are Victorian chaises longues in the bright red kitchen, and a clinically tiled shop setting contrasts with the boisterous wallpaper that decorates the arbitrarily cut-out screens next door. It is as if these fragmented interiors are FAT's way of creating a stage for the staff's craziest ideas. It is, after all, known that in these types of agencies the 'off-the-wall' ideas often mature into bestsellers.

The fit-out, as theatrical as it may appear to the eye, is essentially a common, contemporary office archetype – a multipurpose space solution that promotes the cross-fertilization of ideas. The fact that the KK outlet is open to the public, even on Saturdays, encourages a level of interaction between staff and the public voice that is priceless to the advertising industry. And this open communication is only possible because the design of this workspace leaves all connotations of office and working at the door.

The working environment's entirely bespoke fit-out promotes the company's ethos of communication and has a dramatic visual impact. Nonetheless, all materials used are basic and cost-effective: plywood, vibrant wallpapers, rubber flooring and ceramic tiling. The bold mix of these resources contributes to the fragmented yet identity-driven feel. Mobile furniture units provide necessary flexibility – they can be moved around the office and even out into the gallery space. A 'factory wall' mounted on industrial castors swings out to subdivide the space further, showing that change is an integral facilitator in today's creative working environs.

KK OUTLET

Architect: **Fashion Architecture Taste (FAT)**
Client: **KesselsKramer**
Location: **London, UK**
Completed: **December 2007**
Size: **95 sq m (1,020 sq ft)**
Budget: **undisclosed**

Page 66: The placing of a Victorian chaise longue in a sleek, modern, bright-red kitchen suggests the impact of juxtaposing incongruous elements – a message that is central to KK's creativity.

Left and above: Dramatic contouring and highly patterned wallpaper turn mobile plywood screens into decorative room dividers, which can be moved about to create different configurations of the space, or even folded away.

floor plan

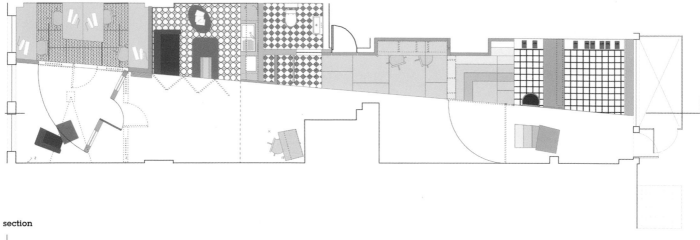

section

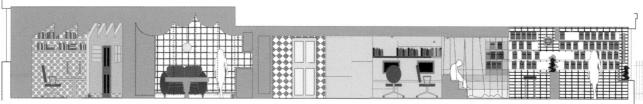

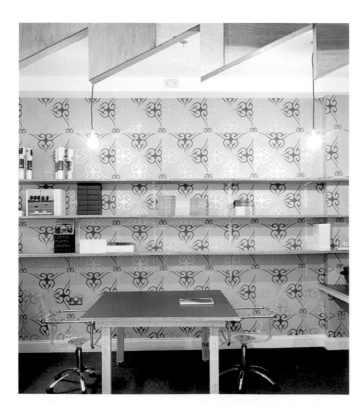

Above: The space is divided in two by an angled wall of plywood. One side is open-plan, the other accommodates a diverse mixture of scenarios. **Left**: The meeting room, with bookshelves set against a wallpapered partition, has a distinctive domestic feel to it.

Opposite: The doors and windows set into the plywood divider create a sense of entering different room settings in a private house.

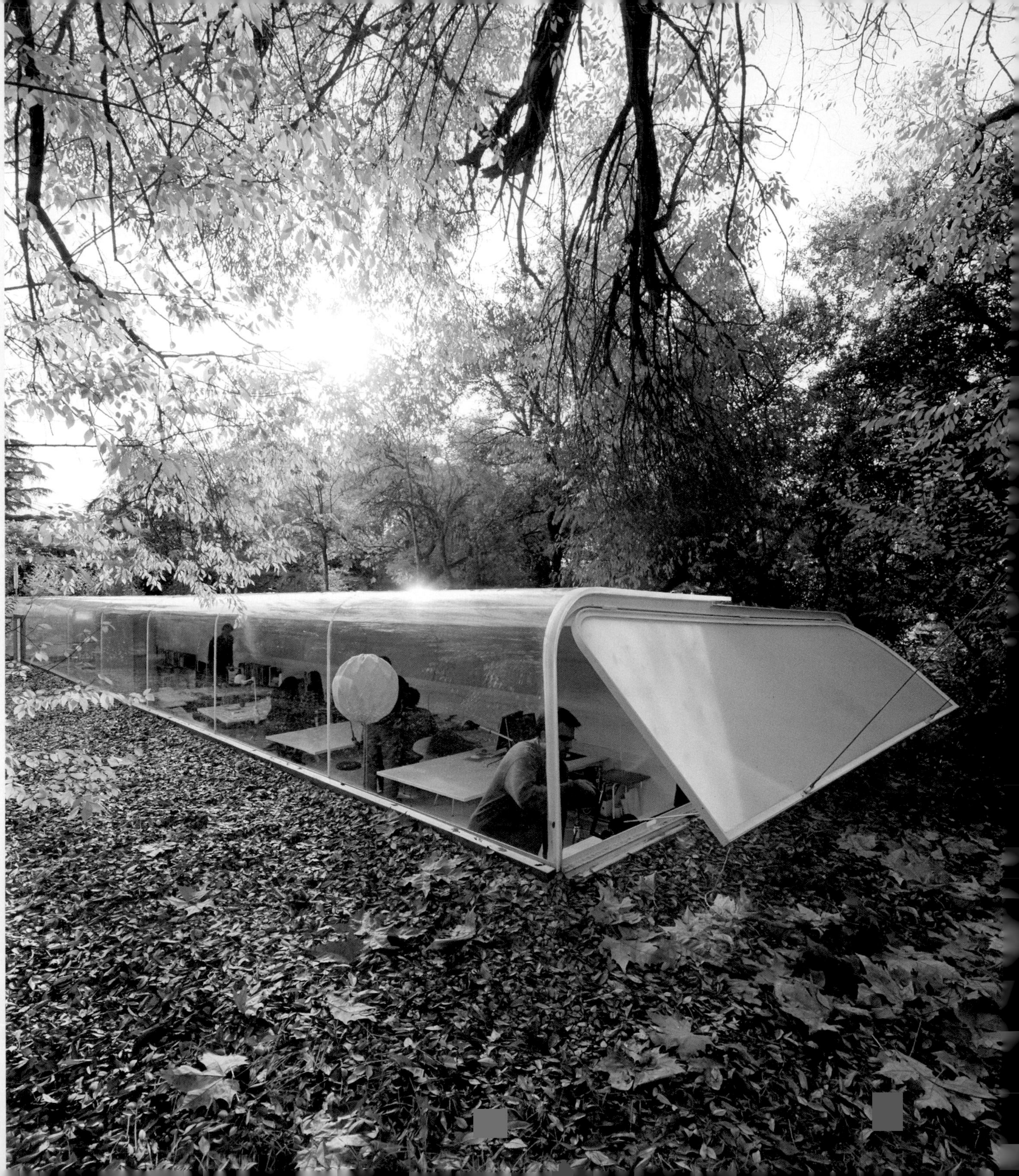

Using nature as inspiration, architects Selgas Cano created for themselves an office in a forest, with a distinctly modern appeal. Having previously worked on domestic projects in similarly leafy surroundings, the husband-and-wife-led team of José Selgas and Lucia Cano set about creating their own workspace, in natural clearings in woodland near Madrid. Part of the 19-metre-long, tubular building is underground. Concrete steps were cut into the earth, leading down to the office entrance, the treads paved with wooden planks. Planning permission was not difficult to obtain in these woods, around 13 km (8 miles) north-west of the Spanish capital. Seemingly simple and inexpensive materials were used in an innovative fashion. The north-facing wall, a 20-mm-thick, curved window, is made of translucent Plexiglas. This plastic panel has milled edges so that silicon sealant could be injected to protect the structure from the elements.

The workstations are housed in the south-facing end of the building. The walls on this side of the office are constructed from fibreglass and polyester, with translucent insulation sandwiched in the middle. This structure offers employees shade from direct sunlight, but also lets in enough light for them to work by. The only concession to artificial light is the odd task light. Otherwise, the leafy canopy above offers enough shade in summer and in winter, when the trees lose their leaves, the structure benefits from as much daylight as possible. The half-dozen employees are very much at one with the elements – from the sound of the rain tapping on the roof to the reliance, for the most part, on the sun for heating the structure. The architects worked closely with suppliers, fitting the building schedule with the availability of materials. For example, the polyester part of one side of the office is made of a material more commonly found on railway carriages; as Selgas Cano required only a small amount of this component, they had to wait for the manufacturer to be asked to fulfil a large order for German railways before they could obtain what they needed.

For natural ventilation, the building has a hinged steel frame, which is opened using a pulley system, operated by a hand-crank; the building's tubular shape encourages air to flow throughout the space. The employees share white-lacquered desks, which are arranged in paired rows and cantilevered from the concrete base of one wall; shelving runs between the

SELGAS CANO STUDIO

Architect: **Selgas Cano Arquitectos**
Client: **Selgas Cano**
Location: **Madrid, Spain**
Completed: **October 2007**
Size: **60 sq m (660 sq ft)**
Budget: **undisclosed**

desks. Floorboards, painted in different colours divide the front part of the building (where the colour is lemon yellow) from the rear (where it is white), and a chartreuse-coloured wall adds a splash of colour to the white, spaceship-like decor.

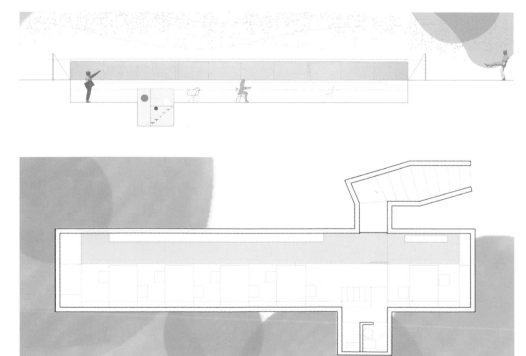

Page 72: A pulley system at one end of the tunnel-like structure provides natural ventilation for the office.

Page 73: The oblong building is designed to exist in harmony with the surrounding forest and blends successfully into the landscape.

Pages 74–75: The 'tunnel' is largely constructed out of translucent Plexiglas, which takes maximum advantage of natural light to illuminate the office.

Above left: The office is located in the middle of a forest outside Madrid.
Above right: The workplace is accessed via concrete steps cut into the earth.
Left: The result of the project is a long and narrow, almost test-tube-like area, which measures 19 metres in length.

Opposite: White-lacquered desks are arranged in pairs along the length of the space, and task lights provide focused additional illumination for each worker.

Japan has a unique standard of construction. Refurbishment is rare and certainly not associated with high design. Most buildings are demolished and rebuilt after only a few years. Martin van der Linden took this fact and turned it on its head for his firm's Tokyo-based office by building it inside out. In an attempt to come up with an environmentally friendly design solution in an industry (construction) that he believes is, by its very nature, the 'antithesis of sustainability', his team spent a lot of time sourcing recycled building materials. The result is a patchwork of materials, some donated, some found, yet all brought back to life in an imaginatively re-created workplace. The main feature is the scraps of a demolished home rebuilt inside out with the original exterior showing on the interior surfaces of the office.

Van der Architects are located in a suburb of Tokyo called Denenchofu, which is exceptional among Japanese cityscapes. It was designed in 1918 according to European town-planning principles, with tree-lined streets and large plots of land, in stark contrast to the densely stacked architecture of Tokyo's other boroughs. Denenchofu's residents are actors, politicians and sports celebrities – not an area where you would expect to find an office. In the midst of the residential villas stands an unusual house, which van der Linden has turned into his firm's office by applying his own workplace design methodology: WorkVitamins.

Following the five distinct steps of WorkVitamins – Initiate, Analyze, Change, Implement and Evaluate – van der Linden wanted his own office to incarnate his methodology. The first step, 'Initiate', means setting a direction, in this case materializing the company's mission statement by counteracting the senseless destruction of intact building materials. A staff member heard about the planned demolition of a 40-year-old house in Kamakura so she asked the contractors whether they could break it down by hand rather than with the usual sledgehammer or bulldozer. In a proactive attempt to salvage the original Japanese sliding doors, window frames and interior features, van der Architects took the house apart and paid the weight of wood in beer.

The second step, 'Analyze', led to the discovery that the back of the planks still had the original contractor's stamps on them. This unusual treatment was soon recognized as a special design feature. Step 3, 'Change', is aimed at creating an office that acts as a catalyst for change. Van der Architects' previous case studies had shown that a

non-office environment encourages people to think 'outside of the box'. Therefore an ideal workplace should read neither like an office nor like a home. The result is a hybrid space, offering a mix of work, live and play components. A central table, for instance, tempts impromptu meetings with a family-style kitchen vibe, and the table football is an important feature, helping staff to let off steam. The company has even started a league for contractors, friends, employees, clients and vendors to mingle, mixing business and socializing in a playful manner. Step 4, 'Implement', led to the decision to create something out of the ordinary – namely, to rebuild the deconstructed house inside out, with the stamps and marks of the original pieces showing. Step 5, 'Evaluate': the workplace makes a clear statement about the custom of throwing things away and always buying new. The novel office proves that even old building materials can be re-erected to form a superior space.

VAN DER ARCHITECTS STUDIO

Architect: **Martin van der Linden**
Client: **van der Architects**
Location: **Tokyo, Japan**
Completed: **August 2008**
Size: **200 sq m (2,150 sq ft)**
Budget: **approx. 150 ml beer/sq m**

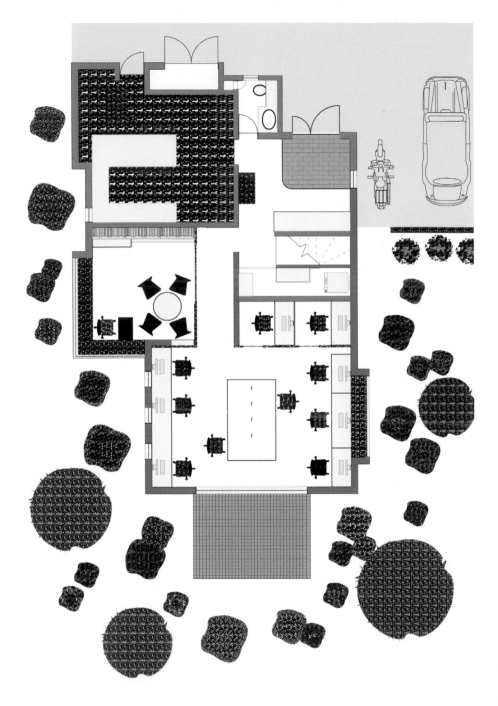

Page 78: To provide a working environment that emphasizes the need for staff to 'think outside the box', the designer erected the walls of an old Japanese house inside the office.

Top: From the outside the office looks like a European house, traditional in design and clad in weatherboarding. **Above left**: In the interior of the building, parts of the demolished Japanese dwelling are set against a skyscape, making a play on the concept of inside/outside. **Right**: The plan highlights the trees and residential character of the building – unusual traits for a Japanese office.

Opposite: Reusing old wood planks gives the office an almost antique feel, especially by Japanese standards.

MEDIUM

(501–2,200 sq m)

When you hear the phrases 'automotive technology' and 'mechanical engineering' your next thought is unlikely to be 'innovative artwork'. Yet the headquarters of Prisma Engineering in Austria can be described as just that. The Frog Queen, as designers SPLITTERWERK call the building, confidently stands on a field in the Steiermark and gives no indication from the outside that it houses cellular offices, the company's R&D programmes for automotive engineering, and a car-testing hall.

SPLITTERWERK remained well within budget by focusing on the general compactness of the building and keeping the surface area minimal. The headquarters, shaped like a cube (18.125 × 18.125 × 17 m), displays a visual playfulness on the exterior walls that continues throughout the building. Apart from the windows, all four walls and the roof are identical. The pixelated square panels of the façade are eye-catching, almost mind-boggling, and their metallic, technical look, references Prisma's industry. The 'pixels' seem to be composed of a range of grey tones, yet when you look closely there are only five patterns in black and white that create ten differently shaded panels. The façade construction plays on the optical illusion of its graphic design. From a distance the building is hard to grasp: it almost seems like a two-dimensional screen hovering in the landscape.

Inside, the artful interior continues to trick the eye: the visual strength of its design suggests an expensive finish. In actual fact, the space simply breaks down into a central atrium constructed of a single surface material (resin), and surrounding cellular offices, each for a maximum of three people, jazzed up with special wallpaper. This straightforward design and layout kept the cost under control. The floors, balustrades, walls and ceilings are painted with an epoxy resin with silver chips and a PUR surface coating. Its silvery reflective surface also makes the space feel bright. All other materials were chosen to minimize maintenance, a request from the client that brings considerable savings in the long run. Even the decorated panels on the façade are easy-to-clean, powder-coated aluminium.

Each office is designed as a 'micro atmosphere', with images of the surrounding Steiermark area printed on the walls. This 'wallpaper' treatment evokes a sense of spring and nature, a clever interpretation of the common 'bringing the outside in' technique, and also a beautiful contrast to Prisma's machine-led engineering. The windows frame the great views and open up the workspace.

PRISMA HEADQUARTERS

Architect/Design: **SPLITTERWERK**
Client: **Prisma Engineering**
Location: **Graz, Austria**
Completed: **November 2007**
Size: **1,400 sq m (15,000 sq ft)**
Budget: **undisclosed**

The arrangement of these windows cleverly plays with the perception of dimension, creating a seemingly complex office design using only two different window shapes. SPLITTERWERK speak of creating a conceptual tension between the narrative of the pictorial interior and the visual effects of the abstract and spatial exterior. But to the clients that visit the Prisma headquarters it will simply be a memorable experience.

Page 84: The views through the windows, cutting into the walls of the meeting rooms at different levels, dovetail with the landscape scenery digitally printed on the walls, creating an original *trompe l'oeil* effect.

Below: The local land- and skyscapes that form the decor on the meeting room walls evoke a sense of freshness and freedom.
Right: Both the counter and the wall in the reception area have the same graphic treatment as the meeting rooms, and the space is lit from above by natural light coming in through the roof.

first floor

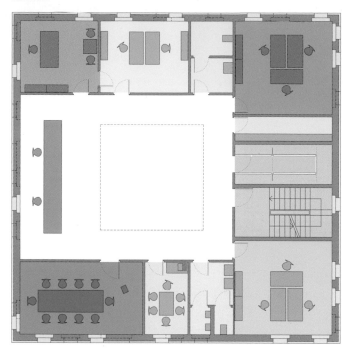

third floor

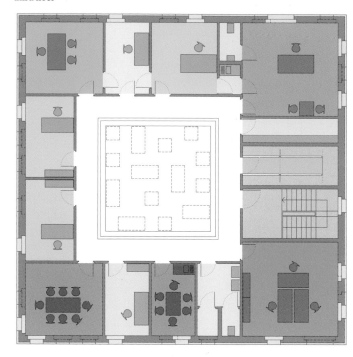

second floor

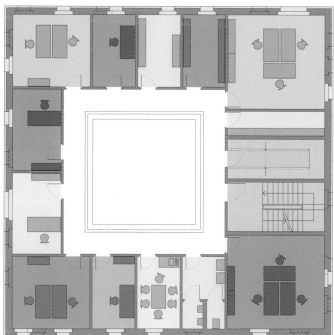

This page: The floor plans show the central atrium is kept free to flood the three floors of the building with light. All meeting rooms and cellular offices are located round the sides of this open column of space.

Opposite: From a distance the façade of the factory resembles a pixelated image – an almost surreal effect that contrasts strongly with the natural visuals in the meeting rooms.

The Hogwarts train in *Harry Potter and the Half-Blood Prince* and the set extensions for key Roman sites in *Angels and Demons* are just two examples of the visual effects the Moving Picture Company (MPC) is famous for creating. The post-production company, a forerunner in the field of colour manipulation in film, is UK-based but needed a new office fit-out for its American headquarters in California. It took on a generic office building in downtown Santa Monica, which Patrick Tighe Architecture converted into a modern office that manifests the essence of MPC's work: light and movement.

Patrick Tighe analysed light studies to explore the nature of light and its relation to colour, and applied a technique derived from this work to the interior. To unite the office's diverse mix of grading rooms, editing bays, tape vaults, conference rooms and client areas, the architects created a dominant design feature that ties the entire office space together – a sinuous spine that weaves its way through the workplace. From it a subsidiary soffit branches off, which houses the company's technological nervous system – the mechanics and the electrics – and connects everything from the computers to lighting back to the equipment room. The spine itself consists of shapes taken from MPC's animations, which are also brought to life in three dimensions on the laser-cut surfaces of the walls. Both the spine and the patterns cut onto the walls create movement in the office and define the interior throughout.

What gives this design its contemporary look is the use of LED lighting, a sustainable and highly efficient mode of illumination. LED fixtures are fitted into custom-made aluminium 'light portals' so that they can be programmed to create various moods through an array of colour settings and intensities. The play of different shades of light becomes even more prominent against the otherwise sleek, monolithic backdrop of Corian surfaces. The LED housings sit flush on the corridor walls but protrude from the surface in the meeting rooms. As requested by the client, the colour schemes are ever-changing. The lighting scheme reinforces the impression of movement, which has influenced MPC's way of working. According to the staff, the motion created by the interior design transmits a sense of flow into their work.

MOVING PICTURE COMPANY OFFICE

Architect: **Patrick Tighe Architecture**
Client: **Moving Picture Company (MPC)**
Location: **Santa Monica, CA, USA**
Completed: **December 2009**
Size: **780 sq m (8,400 sq ft)**
Budget: **US $1.5 million**

Page 90: Sleek surfaces, dramatic forms and the clever use of light make the MPC office look like a movie set from another world.

Below and right: The sculptural, leaning walls, punctured by unframed openings, and the randomly placed light fixtures give the interior a space-age feel.

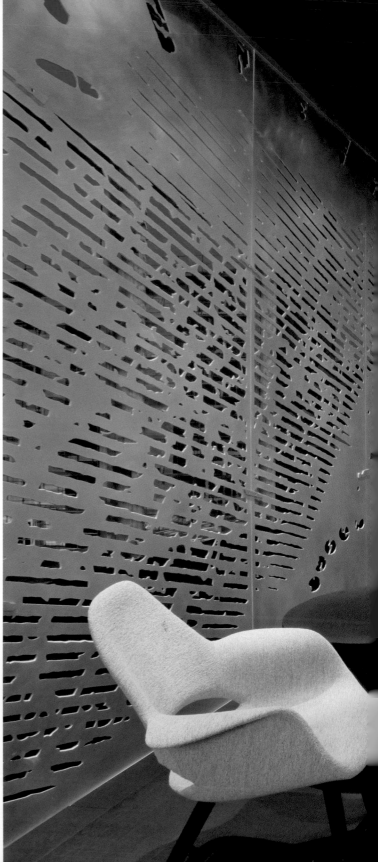

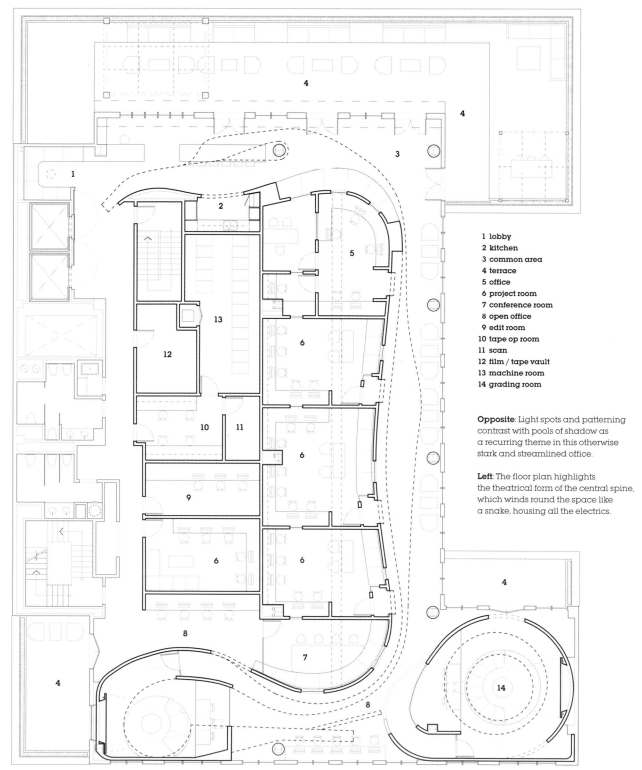

1 lobby
2 kitchen
3 common area
4 terrace
5 office
6 project room
7 conference room
8 open office
9 edit room
10 tape op room
11 scan
12 film / tape vault
13 machine room
14 grading room

Opposite: Light spots and patterning contrast with pools of shadow as a recurring theme in this otherwise stark and streamlined office.

Left: The floor plan highlights the theatrical form of the central spine, which winds round the space like a snake, housing all the electrics.

floor plan

Klab architects were commissioned to transform an existing industrial build into a modern-day office for the media agency F-zein in Athens. The tight budget prompted them to think about local and historical building methods, resulting in an original mix of traditional Greek construction techniques and low-cost materials. The design concept aims to create a sense of 'transparent duality': the office is divided into non-permanent and fixed spaces so that staff feel both part of a team and supported when working autonomously.

The office floor plan shows a space dominated by curves rather than linear structures. Along with the limited use of doors, this is intended to enhance fluidity in F-zein's daily workflow. Curved translucent screens and a grid of galvanized-steel discs that cover the ceiling characterize the open-plan office area and reception. The translucent partitions can be moved around and construct microenvironments for each employee within the larger open space.

Given the economic constraints, klab experimented with corrugated polyester rolls – cheap fibreglass mostly used to shade greenhouses – to create working units. Visually, the material sets a theatrical tone, as its semi-transparent appearance is transformed by changing light throughout the day. The substructure for these screens is made from standard steel scaffolding poles and joints, and can easily be taken down and rebuilt in a variety of configurations. Likewise the galvanized-steel discs that hang from the ceiling are easily dismountable as they have only one central fixing. The discs are a dramatic lighting feature and each contains three laser-cut slots – two filled by long fluorescent light fixtures and the remaining one holds a low-energy bulb. As a result, a whimsical pattern of light appears on the ceiling, which was painted bright orange to contrast with the galvanized metal.

Klab continued to play with colour in the stairway. Here the wall shade gets lighter the further you ascend, and transparent orange Perspex discs hang over the staircase, which tie in with the ceiling design in the main office and create reflections and shadows on the walls.

The most experimental feature of the project was the application of panels of canes to the exterior of the existing building. The traditional Greek method of shading spaces with horizontal canes was reinterpreted by hanging the rods vertically along the building's façade to create a 'second skin' that filters the hot summer sun. The canes

F-ZEIN OFFICE

Architect: **klab architects**
Client: **F-zein**
Location: **Athens, Greece**
Completed: **July 2008**
Size: **750 sq m (8,070 sq ft)**
Budget: **€90,000**

were sourced from a local stream that runs adjacent to the site, and the wild bamboo forms a natural context for the otherwise heavy, industrial complex. Utilizing this eco-friendly feature also meant that klab did not need to install air conditioning to keep the office cool in the heat of the Greek summers. The project shows how tight budgets can help designers rediscover local materials and traditional techniques to create a beautiful and functional office.

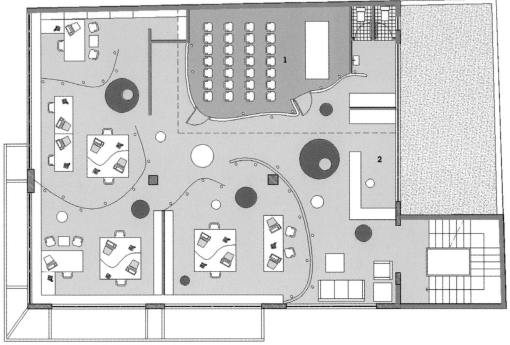

ground floor

1 auditorium
2 reception
3 creative
4 marketing
5 director's office
6 chairman's office
7 secretary
8 conference room

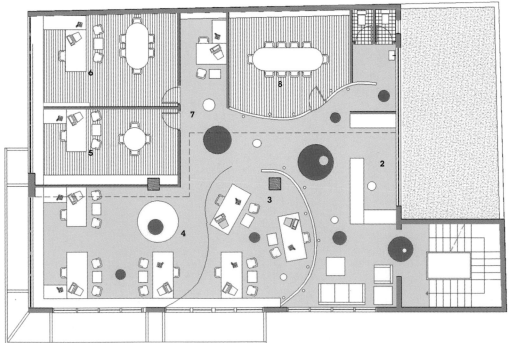

first floor

Page 96: The exterior façade features panels of local cane; the idea was based on the traditional Greek method of creating shade by using cane screens.

This page: The plans show the similar layouts on the two floors: desks are in more or less the same positions and the small auditorium on the ground floor is in the same area as a formal meeting room on the first.

Opposite: Galvanized-steel discs hang from the ceiling – a striking design feature, which doubles as the housing for the light fixtures.

The refurbishment for Digitas of an office in the Saatchi & Saatchi headquarters in London is all about cost-efficiency and future-proofing. The client was looking for a temporary and adaptable space that could accommodate both growth and reduction of staff over time, as well as enable an easy move. As a result, architects 11.04 designed a space that focuses on reducing a sense of permanence, a timely manifestation of the twenty-first-century office reality.

The project is a genuine example of how a low budget can function as a design catalyst. Firstly, the budgetary limitations encouraged 11.04 to look at reusing as many of the existing fittings as possible. Secondly, they sparked a design language that combats the common formalistic approach to office spaces. And thirdly, they led to a stricter than usual validation policy; for instance, each bespoke design fitting is demountable. The objective was to mix long-term thinking with short-term answers.

The prime visual example of this approach is the design of the storage units in the back office. These double up as space dividers and have the look of shipping crates. The units can be closed and moved around the office, or locked and put in store or transported to another location. Even the finish, with its raw joinery and 'non-architectural' detail, is an aesthetic metaphor for the adaptable brief.

Reused features include the flooring. The original flooring was kept on one level and mirrored on the second level, using cheap industrial rubber, for maximum durability. The ceiling, a suspended 1960s solution, was spray-painted in situ after all the damaged tiles had been replaced; this new layer of colour achieved a fresh look.

Even furniture from Digitas's old office is reused, creating an uncoordinated collection and a more informal context for work. New equipment, such as the desks, is juxtaposed with a mix-and-match arrangement of storage units. The decisions made for the design were, ultimately, driven by an ecological awareness that reducing waste is greener than specifying the newest eco products. In addition to the ecological furniture solution, 11.04 persuaded the client not to install air-conditioning units. Instead they were able to activate cross-ventilation from the original classic shallow-plan build by removing all the partitioning units the previous occupants had fitted. And to continue the recycling theme of this frugal fit-out, those partitions were then reused by another company elsewhere in the building.

Meeting room walls were covered in blackboard paint to encourage staff to use them as creative surfaces. Even the monochrome walls in the boardroom purposefully convey a sense of utilitarianism, given their dual function as screens for projector presentations. The fit-out is a timely example of how the colourful and pattern-rich decor of creative agencies in the past decade has been replaced with a utilitarian feel to encourage 'personalization' of office space by staff and through their work.

DIGITAS OFFICE

Architect: **11.04 Architects**
Client: **Digitas**
Location: **London, UK**
Completed: **November 2008**
Size: **1,900 sq m (20,450 sq ft)**
Budget: **£345,000**

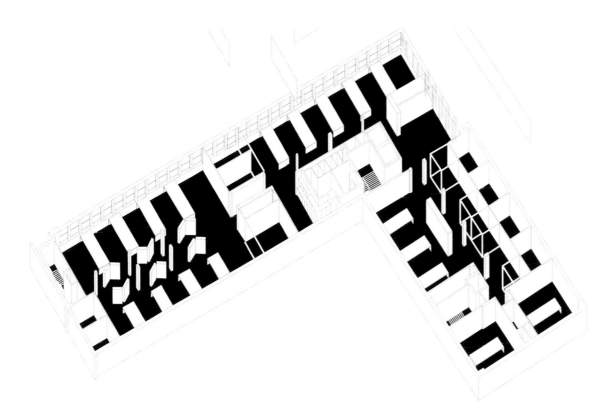

Page 100: Storage units, made from old shipping crates and mounted on castors, can be moved around the office for maximum flexibility – one response on the part of the designers to the brief for a temporary workplace solution.

Opposite: From the dismountable reception desk (*top left*) to the mobile storage units, transience is key to the character of this project, and has the incidental advantage that every member of the staff can personalize their working space.

Above: All the partitioning installed by the preceding occupant of the building was removed and repurposed, leaving one large open-plan space that can be reconfigured at will, using the storage units as screening. **Right**: Painting the walls with blackboard paint was an economical solution to providing space for brainstorming during meetings.

Pages 104–05: The shelving units have a rough finish, which adds to the feeling of a temporary space. Standard desking kept the cost low; each desk can easily be assembled or folded away to increase or decrease workspaces as and when needed.

North of Mexico City lies the historical zone of Querétaro, the location of Nestlé Mexico's new 'competence centre'. This new workplace is set to become the food brand's Latin American flagship for liquid beverages and to operate as a satellite to Nestlé's US headquarters in Ohio.

Nestlé wanted the design to break with the standard look of a manufacturing plant, which focuses mainly on functionality, and instead communicate that it is a laboratory driving innovation in flexible manufacturing.

For this ambitious enterprise Nestlé commissioned Rojkind Arquitectos, a Mexican architecture practice renowned for its original solutions to challenging briefs. The main challenge was overcoming building restrictions imposed by the location: in 1996 Querétaro was declared a UNESCO World Heritage Site. This designation stipulated that any new building – even in the industrial periphery – must include the area's traditional arched portico, the architectural signature of this colonial location.

Rojkind worked with the restriction by reinterpreting both the arch and the portico as key elements of this contemporary construction. The arch, for instance, is redefined as 'a fragment of a dome' and by extension the dome as an amplified arch turning over its own axis. Consequently, Rojkind designed a series of intersecting domes throughout the campus. These became the 'portico', traditionally a walkway with a roof supported by columns, leading up to the entrance of each building. The laboratories are placed within simple box structures, clad in reflective glass. These squares extend out of the spherical domes, in keeping with the geometrical design language. The metallic, opaque exteriors are in striking contrast with the colourful interior walls, which are painted blue, yellow and green. The staff in their white lab coats stands out against the vibrant backdrop of the work setting.

Due to the economic downturn, the budget had to be cut eight times, reducing the floor space from a planned 8,000 sq m down to the final version of 776 sq m, with only three pavilions. Despite some challenging decisions, Rojkind kept the original concept design. They simply scaled down the dimensions without compromising the impact of this original workplace plan.

Costs were kept in check through the choice of affordable materials. A satin glass was used as the skin of each building block. The mirror effect ensures confidentiality, an important requirement given Nestlé's market-leading position. Hybrid lighting makes the project particularly energy efficient. The space between the 'bubbles' and the building roof doubles up as ventilation space, which houses the mechanical, electrical and plumbing works.

Clever space division became especially important when the radical cutbacks on floor area put pressure on efficient space management. Rojkind split each block into three main bodies. The reception and chief manufacturing plant are on the ground floor. A steel staircase then leads to a double-height area that houses the product testing department. On the top floor the so-called 'sensory evaluation lab' is situated, where scientists track colour, texture and viscosity developments.

NESTLÉ LATIN AMERICAN HEADQUARTERS

Architect/Design: **Rojkind Arquitectos, Michel Rojkind**
Client: **Nestlé**
Location: **Querétaro, Mexico**
Completed: **February 2009**
Size: **780 sq m (8,350 sq ft)**
Budget: **undisclosed**

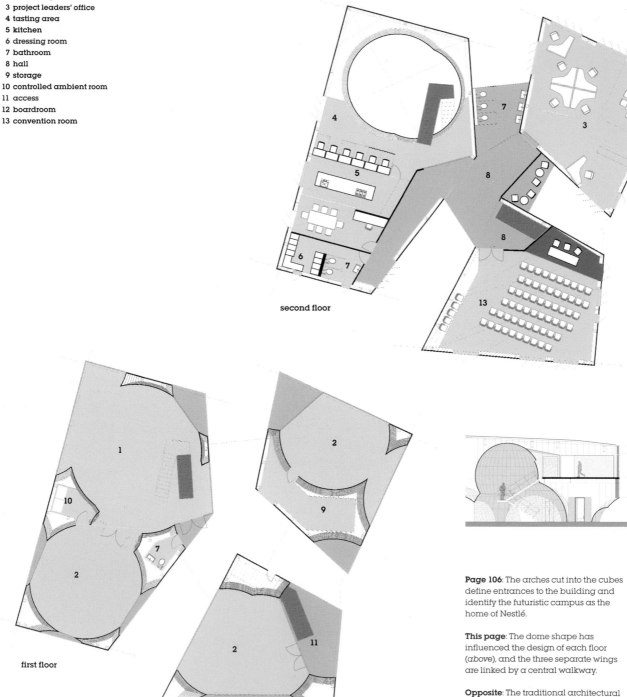

1 prototype floor
2 laboratory
3 project leaders' office
4 tasting area
5 kitchen
6 dressing room
7 bathroom
8 hall
9 storage
10 controlled ambient room
11 access
12 boardroom
13 convention room

second floor

first floor

Page 106: The arches cut into the cubes define entrances to the building and identify the futuristic campus as the home of Nestlé.

This page: The dome shape has influenced the design of each floor (*above*), and the three separate wings are linked by a central walkway.

Opposite: The traditional architectural motif of the arch was a design requirement of this historical site. Rojkind gave it a modern twist and delineated it in a distinctive egg-yolk yellow.

Pages 110–11: Even in the laboratory, the arch, a characteristic feature of local buildings, strongly defines and articulates the space.

This page and opposite: The building and its fittings resemble a spacecraft; the different areas and floors are connected by ladder-like staircases, which create dynamic diagonals in an environment that is strongly defined by horizontal and vertical surfaces.

The concept of an office-cum-showroom has proved popular for many manufacturing firms, but the new headquarters for Mayr-Melnhof, the Austrian wood-processing company, takes this idea to another level. Their expertise in dealing with wood speaks through the entire construction of their office – outside and in. In conjunction with Nussmüller Architekten, the firm have applied the newest wood-processing technology in an innovative way, creating an office that can be used as a reference project for both client and architect.

Established in the nineteenth century, Mayr-Melnhof is a traditional company based in an architecturally conservative part of Austria. Yet the new office manages to close the gap between respecting the local woodland context and projecting itself as a state-of-the-art landmark. Its two oblong wooden boxes connected by a glass structure run alongside a busy highway and seem to float in the air. The wooden constructions are not simply architectural eye candy, they are Nussmüller's response to the initial brief to 'upgrade the location' of the original plant. The site's location next to a federal highway meant noise pollution was an issue. Through elevating the building and placing only the entrance hall, a sound-insulated conference room and the computer facilities on the ground floor, the sound from outside is kept to a minimum.

In a clever and subtle reinterpretation of the outmoded 1980s trend for incorporating company logos into office design, the building itself contains the logo 'MM' in the form of wooden beams that support the two box structures. The wooden façade towers over the roadway, its durable solid larch slats creating a calm and serene effect in deliberate contrast to the continuous flow of traffic. Away from the road the impressive entrance hall opens up over two storeys, offering an airy welcome to all comers. The interior wooden structure is supported by a freestanding wooden installation rather than beams, making the building a clever tribute to the client's passion for bold constructions in wood.

The combination of wood and glass throughout the office rejuvenates the building by evenly juxtaposing light and heavy, open and closed spaces. The entire technical infrastructure is integrated into the wood panels, and a variety of wood surfaces and tones indicate different office zones. For instance, the darker shades of wood stimulate retreat and concentration in the workstations, while lighter finishes encourage communication in the public areas.

MAYR-MELNHOF HEADQUARTERS

Architect: **Nussmüller Architekten**
Client: **Mayr-Melnhof**
Location: **Leoben, Austria**
Completed: **November 2008**
Size: **2,520 sq m (27,160 sq ft)**
Budget: **undisclosed**

From an economic point of view, the vast amount of natural daylight that floods through the glass adds value by keeping the cost of energy down. It also affects the work culture of the company. Despite a continuing preference in Teutonic cultures for cellular offices, Nussmüller, collaborating with office furniture company Bene, have provided a flexible interior, aided by the glass partitions. Single, two-person and open-plan desk arrangements are easily established, and the glass interfaces make each office and person feel part of the larger whole.

A pine tree in the central atrium is a reminder of the client's fascination with wood and the importance of this wonderful natural resource. And the cost efficiency of using local wood enabled the construction to complete within ten months. The Mayr-Melnhof headquarters perfectly demonstrate that contemporary architecture does not have to break with conventions – it can simply reinvent them.

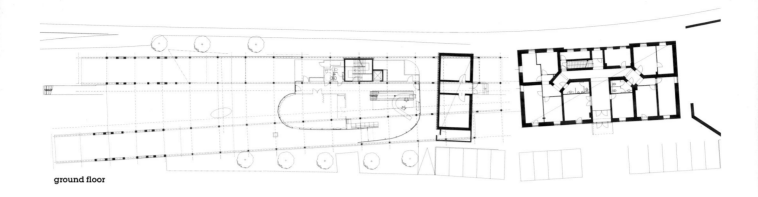

ground floor

layout of first and second floor

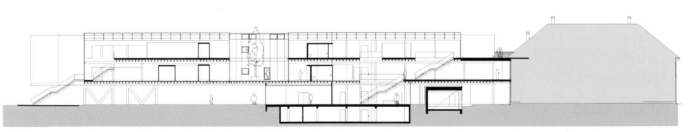

section through old and new building

Page 114: The wooden structure supporting the building forms the client's initials, MM (for Mayr-Melnhof).

This page: Like a cruise ship, the extension 'embarks' from the original warehouse.

Opposite: The bright café has large picture windows that make the most of the spectacular view of the surrounding landscape.

Pages 118–19: Inside, the use of glass allows long views through the building, so that all the working areas are connected. Furniture is kept low to promote this transparency and to encourage communication.

When the healthcare marketing agency Langland commissioned a revamp of their offices in the gracious town of Windsor, known chiefly for its royal castle and park, they wanted a space that said neither 'healthcare' nor 'tradition'. The company chose Jump Studios for their notoriously striking design style and ability to achieve impact with a limited budget. As is common when working with restricted finances, the key was to identify which elements to prioritize in what Jump calls a 'hierarchical' approach to design. Ceilings, bathrooms, even break-out areas were left untouched or given a standard finish. Instead the design focused on one element that characterizes the whole workspace: a central spine that mirrors the odd curve of the building.

The spine is essentially the lifeline of the company, and represents an inversion of the existing layout of the Langland office. For an open-plan centre, with meeting rooms and cellular offices around the periphery, Jump substituted a backbone housing the company's hardware and technology, plus central functions like the post room, library, meeting rooms, break-out booths, magazine archives, tea points and reception. This backbone offers a 'plug-in' capability: seats, storage, tabletops – almost any piece of furniture – can be added or removed easily.

By centralizing the main office elements and letting the open-plan space flow around it, Jump have cleverly tied in the architectural layout with the workflow. Collections of magazines and product samples encourage staff to leave their desks and move towards the central resource for non-digital inspiration. The building's curved shape helps to introduce a dynamic of browsing, standing and sitting, which draws staff together.

The central spine acts as both a divider and a connector. It separates the accountants from the creative workforce for better concentration. At the same time, it visually connects the different zones and generates an effective circulation pattern. The prefabricated plug-in system has future-proofed the space: it can now adapt to any given set-up due to its flexible nature. Aesthetically, the spine projects a distinct character with the white tiles subtly evoking connotations of cleanliness and hygiene appropriate to the healthcare industry. A bold contrast with these associations with a bathroom or a swimming pool is achieved by the soft upholstery in bright-green tweed, which at very least offers a talking point to staff and clients alike. As the materials used to create this striking effect of

LANGLAND OFFICES

Architect: **Jump Studios**
Client: **Langland**
Location: **Windsor, UK**
Completed: **December 2008**
Size: **930 sq m (10,010 sq ft)**
Budget: **£800,000**

form and colour were relatively inexpensive, the spine is a fine example of Jump's 'big impact, small investment' approach.

The rest of the space sports an atmospheric play between diversified working environments, brought to life by a mixture of hybrid styles. The open-plan office feels like a cool, modern creative lab; the client-facing rooms have the air of a private members' club through the use of both luxury and domestic textures; and the social break-out areas are relaxed and laid back – for example, the library shines in warm copper and the canteen imitates an outdoor feel with its picnic-style bench. The floor throughout is grey linoleum, which is both environmentally friendly and aesthetically pleasing.

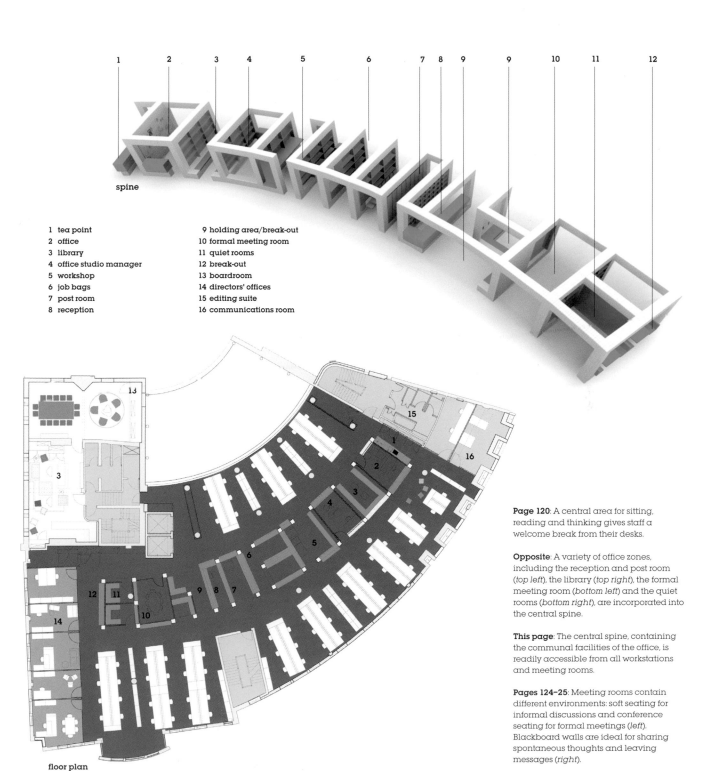

spine

1 tea point
2 office
3 library
4 office studio manager
5 workshop
6 job bags
7 post room
8 reception

9 holding area/break-out
10 formal meeting room
11 quiet rooms
12 break-out
13 boardroom
14 directors' offices
15 editing suite
16 communications room

floor plan

Page 120: A central area for sitting, reading and thinking gives staff a welcome break from their desks.

Opposite: A variety of office zones, including the reception and post room (*top left*), the library (*top right*), the formal meeting room (*bottom left*) and the quiet rooms (*bottom right*), are incorporated into the central spine.

This page: The central spine, containing the communal facilities of the office, is readily accessible from all workstations and meeting rooms.

Pages 124–25: Meeting rooms contain different environments: soft seating for informal discussions and conference seating for formal meetings (*left*). Blackboard walls are ideal for sharing spontaneous thoughts and leaving messages (*right*).

This multidisciplinary design practice has transformed a mini-mall in Los Angeles into a modern, non-hierarchical studio space. As well as project space for the firm, part of the building is given over to the practice's notNeutral product line and space for tenants, including for a salon, a café and a retail outlet.

The designers took down the external walls, replacing a hotchpotch of design styles – from Spanish revival to art deco – with a single system of glass and metal screens; these are decorated with a motif featuring Triton, the Greek god of the sea, referencing the building's former use as a swimming pool. On the first floor the new walls accommodate exterior balconies, converting them into screened porches. The pitch of the roof has been levelled off, while preserving an existing skylight, and this streamlining, along with the installation of additional skylights, creates the desired light and airy southern California effect.

Existing timber beams and concrete flooring were retained and ductwork was left exposed to add to the neutral colour palette. The use of foil at the ceiling's centre enhances the building's industrial feel while at the same time echoes Andy Warhol's famous studio suggesting that the office is an 'ideas factory' where things are conceived and created.

The main entrance leads to a reception. Here, an indoor park has been created underneath the staircase by covering the top of a metre-high platform with artificial turf – a gesture to the firm's landscape practice. This reference spreads throughout the office: the same material is used as an accent in the bathrooms.

A large, open conference room, with floor-to-ceiling sliding glass doors, is adjacent to the reception area. It contains two long conference tables with white tabletops, surrounded by wood and steel chairs. A kitchen featuring notNeutral products is situated around the corner. The staircase wall leading up to the first floor is used as a display space for projects past, present and future.

Instead of separate studio spaces for the various disciplines – interior design, architecture, urban planning – the office houses pods of six to nineteen individual workstations. These were deployed for maximum flexibility and to enable collaboration, as well as creating a non-hierarchical environment. Three small conference rooms are also upstairs, one referred to as the tree house because it overlooks a large tree and lets the greenery indoors.

RIOS CLEMENTI HALE STUDIOS OFFICE

Architect: **Rios Clementi Hale Studios**
Client: **Rios Clementi Hale Studios**
Location: **Los Angeles, CA, USA**
Completed: **December 2008**
Size: **1,580 sq m (17,000 sq ft)**
Budget: **undisclosed**

In addition to the fact that this workspace reuses an old building and is part of the rejuvenation of an up-and-coming neighbourhood, Rios Clementi Hale were also keen to reuse materials: for example, they fabricated a communal lunch table from leftover wood taken from the original mini-mall site.

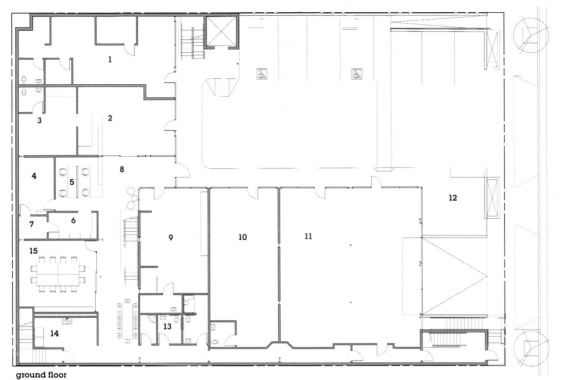

ground floor

1 salon
2 notNeutral
3 storage
4 filing
5 reception
6 mail room
7 server
8 lobby
9 model shop
10 retail
11 restaurant
12 outdoor deck
13 bathrooms
14 kitchen
15 conference room
16 balcony
17 office
18 print/copy
19 library

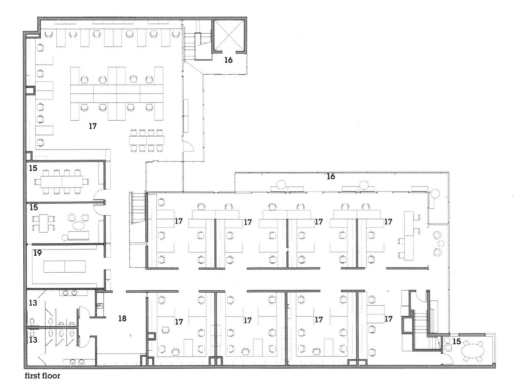

first floor

Page 126: Glass and metal screens use a motif that references Triton, the Greek messenger of the sea – a nod to the building's former use as a swimming pool.

Above: The new floor plate combines work areas – such as the conference room – with public spaces – such as the retail space and restaurant – enabling the building to function well both as an architectural practice and a product showroom. **Left**: With the exception of two enclosed meeting rooms, the second floor is predominantly open plan, an approach that makes good use of space and encourages collaborative working.

Opposite: The office showcases the architectural practice's product line notNeutral.

Opposite: Sliding glass doors let in the southern Californian sunlight.

Above left: The architects stripped back the surface of the building to reveal the service infrastructure, such as this ductwork. **Above right:** There is ample wall space to display the practice's work. **Left:** The architects removed the hotchpotch of design styles to create a well-connected work environment with good visibility from all around the office.

Platoon Kunsthalle/Graft + Baik Jiwon 134/135

Founded in Berlin in 2000, Platoon works to promote subcultural movements in areas such as street art, fashion, new media arts, music and political engagement. Its trademark was the shipping-container architecture of its Berlin office. The trend for using containers as workspaces has spread all over Europe, with examples such as Urban Splash's 'container city' in London celebrating the temporary nature of this construction solution. Modular container systems were renowned for being cheap and quick to install but also notoriously 'tinny' – they lacked the comfort of a serious working environment. Today, in times when reducing expenditure is a top priority and temporary working set-ups are commonplace, it is no surprise to see the container concept reborn with an up-to-date twist.

Platoon recently opened a subsidiary in Seoul to extend its subcultural development programme to Asia. Echoing the signature style of modules stacked on top of each other, Platoon again chose to use containers as the main construction element – twenty-eight ISO cargo containers in total. But to ensure a progressive approach for the Korean building, they brought in Graft architects and Baik Jiwon to develop the concept of flexible architecture as a global phenomenon even further.

The brief was to design a transient, adaptable space. Nothing illustrates that aspect better than the containers themselves, so the designers focused on highlighting the office's shell, using dramatic lighting and a lavish surface treatment. The arrangement of the containers also differentiates this multipurpose workplace from previous models. The boxes, which house offices, restaurants, a library and artists studios, are densely stacked to form an integrated whole.

One side of the stacked containers opens to the street with floor-to-ceiling glass windows, a far cry from the earlier claustrophobic container interiors. The walls facing the centre core have been removed in most containers to open up the space, creating a lofty workplace with generous windows and high ceilings. While the container look is preserved on the outside, the interior has been given a significant upgrade. The walls are covered in aluminium sheets that function as thin wallpaper and create a mirror effect. This considerably widens the rooms and makes for a bright and engaging workplace. In keeping with the container theme, all of the surfaces are intended to bear marks and scratches as a result of people working there, thus emphasizing the rawness of the construction.

PLATOON KUNSTHALLE

Architect: **Graft + Baik Jiwon**
Client: **Platoon**
Location: **Seoul, South Korea**
Completed: **March 2009**
Size: **920 sq m + 120 sq m roof terrace (9,910 sq ft + 1,250 sq ft)**
Budget: **US $2 million**

The budget was tight and the initial plan to add a further floor to the site had to be reworked. But the choice of containers seems to be resourceful when material cost, construction time and the eventual cost of demolition are taken into account. The main ecological feature of the project is its ephemeral character – the fact that it can be easily moved or removed. The architects have responded to the current property climate by basing its construction on the temporary use of real estate. The location of the building itself in Seoul city also adds an interesting dimension: it sits in a prestigious part of town among commercial galleries and luxury brand stores. The unrefined container look plays on that tension and interaction between the two colliding worlds of subculture and commerce.

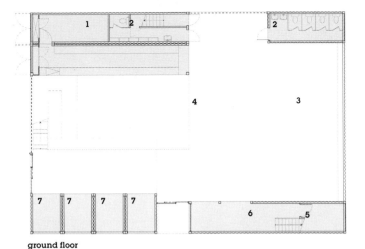

ground floor

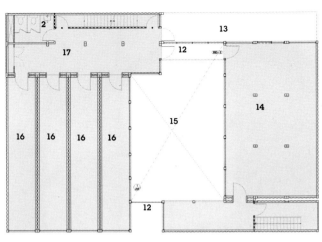

second floor

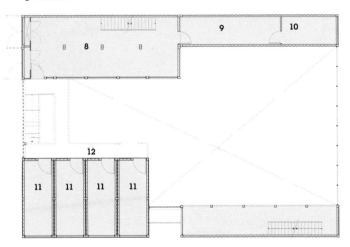

first floor

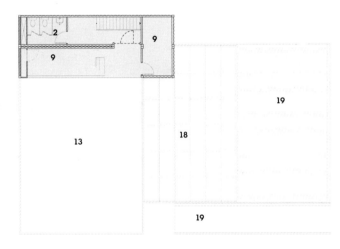

third floor

1 kitchen
2 bathroom
3 LED screen
4 lounge
5 boiler room
6 reception/shop
7 exhibition space
8 multipurpose room
9 storage/tech room
10 MDF room
11 artist residence
12 balcony
13 patio
14 multipurpose room/
   conference room
15 open space
16 office
17 hall
18 skylight
19 roof

Page 132: In total, twenty-eight stacked cargo containers house this office and event space in Seoul.

Opposite: A canteen for all staff members has a shipyard aesthetic, created by the steel container walls and a staircase that might take passengers on board a cruise ship.

Above: Each of the four levels configures the constituent containers differently, creating an inventive and varied series of spaces that shows how versatile the basic component is.

This page: The glass-window front allows passers-by to see into the space and also brightens the interior. But despite the ample supply of daylight, overhead illumination is still needed throughout, enhancing the raw, industrial style of the offices.

Opposite: The sofas slot into each other, mirroring the container stacking on a micro level.

We are proud
to be part of
the EDF Group

Welcome to EDF Energy, part of EDF Group

We produce, distribute and supply the power that is the lifeblood of the communities we serve. But its production currently depletes precious resources and creates carbon dioxide emissions that cause climate change.

The nation needs secure and affordable energy to prosper, but without harming the climate.

We must lead the energy change.

We will build on our position as the largest generator of low-carbon electricity in Britain and Europe and we will accelerate our efforts to provide sustainable energy solutions that will decarbonise homes, businesses and transport.

Sustainability isn't just part of our business. It's the heart of our business.

Welcome to low carbon Britain

eDF ENERGY

Energy supplier EDF has impeccable green credentials, and its new office fit-out in London's Victoria was the ideal way to show them off, through the use of recycled materials and new company branding. The task began in the reception. Before the redesign, visitors entered the main building and then went up to the first floor, where there was little in the way of a meet-and-greet experience; now there is a dedicated concierge-style reception service, with a light installation that gives details of EDF's green initiatives. The flooring here is reclaimed timber from the Hoxton Square Gallery, where materials from artists' work are given out free for reuse. The introduction of turnstiles into the entrance area has made the office more secure.

As EDF Energy has a large number of visitors, BDGworkfutures created a dedicated 'touchdown zone' for their exclusive use. Here visitors, either colleagues from other offices or external guests, can plug in their laptops, check their emails and work between meetings in order to minimize the time wasted in travelling. This is a designated area for visitors – regular members of staff are not allowed to use it – so they do not feel they are encroaching on staff space.

To promote a better circulatory route around the office, there are now new manifestations (markings to aid the visibility of glass sheets in the office) using icons from EDF's plan to reduce carbon emissions in ten steps. After a space-utilization study had identified that there were too many large meeting spaces, the floor plate was reconfigured to offer an increased number of smaller meeting rooms, which were given a crisper finish and adapted to provide more informal places to gather.

One of the key green measures undertaken in this workspace was to reuse 70% of the existing furniture. New tops were added to the tables, task chairs were reupholstered and storage units were resprayed. Ceiling tiles were also kept and the air-conditioning system retained but refurbished to improve its output.

Printers and copiers are now centralized to reduce paper usage and oblige staff to move around the office more. The worktops in these service centres are made from 100% yogurt-pot tops. All of the manufacturers used were vetted for their sustainable credentials – even the firm that supplied the carpet tiles has a 'cradle-to-cradle' approach. Elsewhere, the flooring is hardwearing rubber and coconut-fibre rope. Other sustainable materials used in the project include cork for the pin-boards outside the meeting rooms. During the fit-out itself, as much as possible

EDF ENERGY OFFICE

Architect: **BDGworkfutures**
Client: **EDF Energy**
Location: **London, UK**
Completed: **June 2009**
Size: **1,800 sq m (19,380 sq ft)**
Budget: **undisclosed**

of the waste generated by the demolition was saved from going to the landfill site by reuse and recycling.

Sustainability is key in every detail of this project, which is what makes it an exemplary green office. Inks used on the graphics and manifestations are water-based and contain no solvents, and ceramic mugs have been substituted for plastic cups in the break-out area. Recycling options have been beefed up: now office workers can dispose separately of plastic cups, aluminium cans, white paper, general plastics and confidential documents for the correct method of processing.

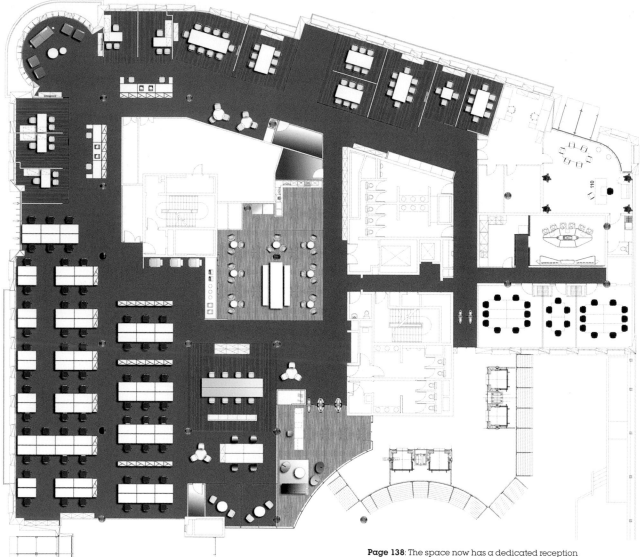

Page 138: The space now has a dedicated reception area, which has simultaneously improved brand identity and the security of the premises.

Above: The architects and EDF configured the main office area to give each desk an equal amount of space; a variety of meeting rooms and areas run along the sides of the building.

Opposite: Part of the brief was to incorporate EDF's branding in the new design so that it figured strongly but subtly (*top left*). Graphical illustrations on the walls show the client's environmental commitments (*top right*). In the response to the results of a space utilization study, the architects decided to provide many small meeting rooms rather than a few infrequently used large ones (*bottom left*). The office was reconfigured to provide a better circulatory route for staff and visitors (*bottom right*).

Step 2

Helping our
customers to
change – at home
and at work

Step 3

Decarbonising
heating

Sustainability isn't part of our business. It's the heart of our business.

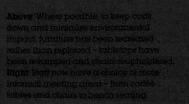

Above Where possible, to keep costs down and minimize environmental impact furniture has been recreated rather than replaced – tabletops have been revamped and chairs reupholstered. **Right** Staff now have a choice of more informal meeting areas – from coffee tables and chairs to bench seating.

Bottega + Ehrhardt transformed a loft space in the centre of Stuttgart into an office for the advertising agency Publicmotor. The architects' aim was to divide up the space into several distinct zones, making a clear statement in each one. Visitors enter the office by passing through what is first glimpsed as a 'forest' of triangular, dark-coloured three-dimensional shapes. If, however, visitors view them from the other side it becomes clear they are an arrangement of LCD monitors, showing aspects of Publicmotor's work. The entrance is deliberately presented in a theatrical way in order to reference the agency's involvement in the arena of film. At the same time, the idea of movement is very important to draw visitors into the space. Bottega + Ehrhardt were influenced by the public sculptures of the architect Luis Barragán in Mexico City, which are very tall, coloured triangular concrete structures.

In the next zone, rectangular volumes, which are covered in a light-grey carpet and have integrated lighting, divide the space into separate workstations. They also act as sound mufflers. The space is relatively large for the number of permanent employees, usually between six and eight, but Publicmotor also employs a large number of freelancers who require workspaces. The design responds to this need for flexibility by hiding workplaces behind the carpet-covered structures. This means that the scale of the office is never compromised, but it never feels empty. This impression is important to Publicmotor – having a workspace that seems empty, and where there do not appear to be many people working, could send out the wrong message to visiting clients. This idea is particularly pertinent during times of economic uncertainty.

The workstations for the management and also the meeting rooms are divided by dramatic floor-to-ceiling glass partitions. These can be individually modified by pulling bronze-coloured semi-transparent curtains across the space.

Yellow vertical volumes serve as units housing the office's library and separate the working area from the communications zone. A long wooden table, where the staff come together to eat, is in an area connected to a small kitchen at the back of the office. A service zone containing the agency cutting-rooms and also bathrooms can be found behind a carpet-covered wall. A white polyurethane floor throughout the office helps to emphasize the openness of the space.

PUBLICMOTOR OFFICE

Architect: **Bottega + Ehrhardt**
Client: **Publicmotor Brand Communication**
Location: **Stuttgart, Germany**
Completed: **2008**
Size: **700 sq m (7,540 sq ft)**
Budget: **undisclosed**

The whole design strikes a balance between the cool colours – the whites and greys – and the warmer more atmospheric elements – the lustrous bronze shades, the wooden tables and the suspended textile lights.

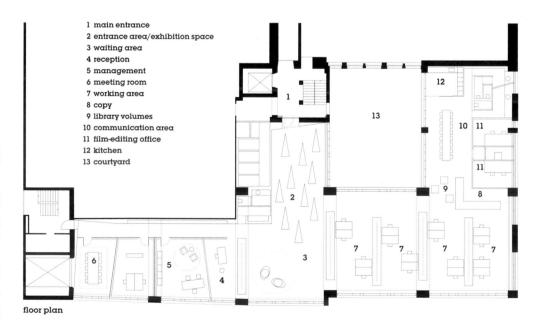

1 main entrance
2 entrance area/exhibition space
3 waiting area
4 reception
5 management
6 meeting room
7 working area
8 copy
9 library volumes
10 communication area
11 film-editing office
12 kitchen
13 courtyard

floor plan

Page 144: The series of dark-coloured volumes that greet the visitor (shown at number 2 on the plan) are deliberately theatrical and dramatic – a reference to the client's work in film.

Above left: The whiteness of the project gives it a certain futuristic feel, as if it were on the set of a sci-fi film. **Above right**: Storage units have a sculptural quality to them. **Left**: The workstations, shown on the bottom right of the plan, are placed between long, rectangular volumes; each one has a generous amount of space around it.

Opposite: The space needed to be flexible to accommodate the varying number of casual staff employed by the agency.

Page 148: Suspension lights, at different heights within the design scheme, add spatial interest to the office.

Page 149: Where the design might feel clinical, elements such as the warm grey screening soften the harsher tones and provide a colour balance.

This workplace is the new home for designers Studio Gang, who were both architect and client on this project. Studio Gang converted an original 1920s office, which looked like a private detective agency, into an open and light contemporary workspace, while innovatively reusing many original materials and features.

The partitions dividing the space into small, sectioned-off offices, along with over twenty patterned-glass doors and transoms, were removed to provide a more open space. The doors were subsequently deployed as divider walls for three separate conference rooms. In the large central kitchen, wooden tables accommodate communal dining, as well as providing a place to hold office-wide meetings. The aim of the floor plan was to open up the office visually and spatially. This part of the design embodies the firm's principles of creative collaboration, communication and environmental consciousness.

A new outdoor courtyard, which is accessible from the kitchen, functions as a vent shaft for the office, supplying air to the workspace and creating more light thanks to the whitewashed surface. On warmer days it also provides the perfect outdoor meeting spot to entertain clients or brainstorm ideas. Crucial to this design brief was a desire to create an interior that had spatial variety to engage and inspire the staff. A wall of windows runs down the length of the office, the intention being to reconfigure the working environment so that each room has a view of the city and direct access to daylight.

Elsewhere, vintage materials were put to new uses in order to reduce the amount of waste produced by the project. For example, marble wainscoting that previously lined the central corridor was used for countertops, desks and tables, while the office's reception desk and lunchroom are constructed from salvaged wood. Other items of furniture have been reupholstered in grey fabric and given a new lease of life.

Sustainability in this workplace goes further than recycling materials and reducing the use of applied finishes, however. Studio Gang has installed energy-efficient lighting and water-conservation systems, and special care was taken in the workshop to filter and exhaust air to maintain good air quality.

The refit was something of a labour of love for the architects, and the careful redeployment of what was there before was not achieved overnight. The project was built over two years: the first year focused on overhauling the workspace, and in the second year the bathrooms and kitchens were renovated.

WORKSPACE 1212

Architect: **Studio Gang**
Client: **Studio Gang**
Location: **Chicago, IL, USA**
Completed: **August 2007**
Size: **680 sq m (7,300 sq ft)**
Budget: **US $78,000**

1 reception
2 conference room
3 open office
4 office/library
5 reference/printing area/hub
6 archive
7 shop
8 materials lab
9 kitchenette
10 studio café
11 garden courtyard

Page 150: The space dates back to the 1920s and the architects wanted to leave some original elements that would merge with the more modern features, such as these pieces of contemporary furniture.

This page: The office was transformed from a heavily partitioned space into an airy, open-plan environment with an outdoor meeting area incorporated into the building's perimeter.

Opposite: An open-plan space was essential for this project as it helps to generate collaborative working (*top right*). Meeting rooms have glass doors, providing a visual connection to the rest of the office (*top left*). They also feature significant storage (*bottom right*). The new outdoor courtyard, accessed from the kitchen, provides an al fresco dining and meeting area (*bottom left*).

floor plan

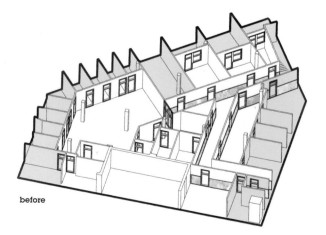

before

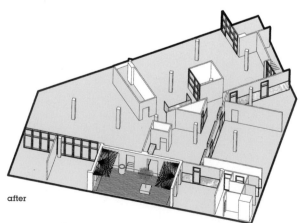

after

Pullpo's offices are located in an abandoned salt factory in the west of Santiago, Chile. The design had to balance the industrial aesthetic with the requirements of a modern advertising agency who represent a range of cool brands.

The project includes offices, conference rooms, photographic studios, service and storage areas, a cafeteria, bathrooms and parking. Architect Hania Stambuk felt it was necessary to keep the design balanced by keeping objects on a human scale in the massive building that once housed large-scale industrial processes. The new architectural interventions were harnessed to the original structure, though some areas of the office were adapted and restored more than others. For instance, utilities such as lavatories obviously had to be updated to comply with modern standards.

Stambuk created a series of flexible units that can play host to all the needs of the advertising agency. The units are structurally joined by steel cables, which are anchored to the existing factory trusses. The prefabricated system is a low-cost design approach and resembles a Meccano set. Materials that enabled quick assembly were used here – steel, glass and Isopol panels. These panels are made out of prefabricated polyurethane sheet wrapped in tin, and have high thermal capacity (they are manufactured for use in refrigeration); they are also versatile, lightweight and easy to disassemble and move around. Flexibility is key as Pullpo's work involves a diverse range of activities – from meeting clients to photo shoots. Photographing the agency's work formed a unique part of the project. The images generated, together with the greenery planted around inside the office, add a surrealist element to the workspace. Part of the brief was to explore the idea that advertising can surpass reality and that the aim is to create astonishment.

Each unit in the former factory space allows services such as temperature and ventilation to be localized for the comfort of the employees. Light fittings are quite bare, which complements the raw appearance of the office, and stark strip lighting has been used in the car park.

This series of cells or 'citadels' is intended to suggest that the creative process is like an 'assembly line' of ideas, and perhaps another reference to the building's industrial past. The arrangement not only allows for the maximum structural capacity, but also creates an interesting aesthetic juxtaposition between old and new. And it makes the building a moody and atmospheric place to work.

PULLPO CREATIVE LAB

Architect: **Hania Stambuk**
Client: **Gonzales Silva and Gabriel Schkolnick**
Location: **Santiago, Chile**
Completed: **2008**
Constructed area: **670 sq m (7,230 sq ft)**
Budget: **£150,000**

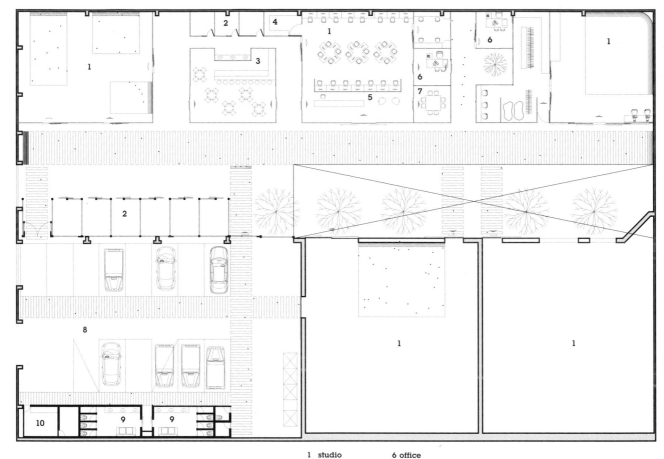

1 studio	6 office
2 cell	7 meeting room
3 canteen	8 parking
4 archive	9 bathroom
5 reception	10 security

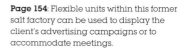

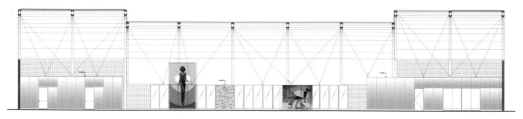

Page 154: Flexible units within this former salt factory can be used to display the client's advertising campaigns or to accommodate meetings.

Above: The arrangement of the different areas and the large studios give the space the flexibility to adapt to Pullpo's various activities, which include photo shoots and liaising with clients. The trees, planted in the corridor, add to the bizarre feel of the space. **Left**: The large office includes an indoor car parking area; its design incorporates the building's original curved ceiling.

Opposite: New units, which are low-cost and easy to assemble, give a human scale to what is otherwise a cavernous industrial space.

Australian architects Geyer wanted to transform their offices in Melbourne into a flexible workspace that fosters both internal and external collaboration, to aid the studio in developing its emerging international brand. There is no traditional reception. Instead, there is a welcome area, effectively a 'hotelling' environment, that is capable of accommodating numerous groups of people and hosting large functions. There is no separation between the public/client space and the workspace: everything is on show in one big studio, where every function – from client meetings to internal gatherings or casual conversations around the coffee pot – is out in the open. The intention is to cultivate energy and the sharing of knowledge through increased visual transparency. This idea is played out in the form of a mirrored box, which sits in a sunken area furnished with a mixture of classic and contemporary styles. The mirrored box reflects the space around it and thus becomes almost invisible.

Opposite this welcome zone is the 'generator' – an open-plan zone where the walls are lined with trade literature and material samples. The collection can be reached via a powder-coated industrial ladder. The walls along the main corridor have surfaces designed so that work in progress can be easily pinned up and displayed and this can generate impromptu brainstorming sessions.

The open-plan workspace is clustered into zones, which maximize natural daylight and are identified by the different colours that punctuate the perimeter walls. When the temperature is below 24°C the air conditioning is switched off; if need be, windows and doors (which include those of the original façade) are opened to allow cross-ventilation. The rear deck of the office even provides an al fresco dining spot.

Geyer have used a number of sustainable solutions, in accordance with their belief that 'what's good for the environment is good for business'. Materials used include woven eco-panels, carpets made by Interface (an environmentally responsible company) and reused blackbutt timber panelling for the walls and floors. The reuse of existing classic pieces of furniture and some joinery was key to achieving cost-effectiveness in the scheme. The tea point from the previous office was left so that plumbing and electrics did not have to be altered.

The fitments and furnishings are all mobile and, every quarter Geyer moves the large pedestals within the studio around to re-energize the space. This can be done extremely quickly, minimizing the downtime. The overall aim of this workplace design project was to drive design ideas and discussion, and also for guests to feel the energy and be part of the creation of amazing environments.

GEYER OFFICE

Architect: **Geyer**
Client: **Geyer**
Location: **Melbourne, Australia**
Completed: **March 2007**
Size: **560 sq m + 130 sq m deck (5,970 sq ft + 1,400 sq ft)**
Budget: **AUS $685,000**

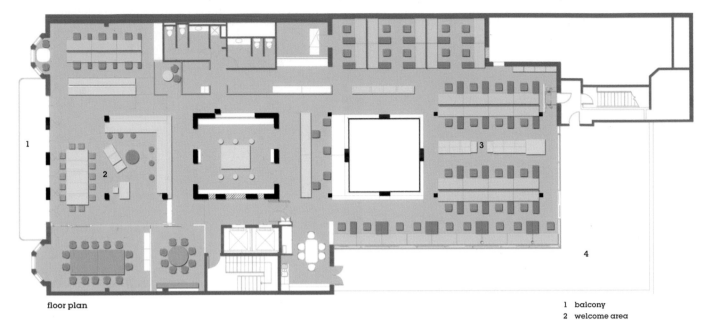

floor plan

1 balcony
2 welcome area
3 work zone
4 outdoor decking

Page 158: A generous provision of informal meeting space is a key factor in fostering good communication between staff.

Above: The concept of 'hotelling' informed this design: workers, clients and visitors all have access to the entire space and can enter any part of it. There is no conventional reception area, instead there is a 'welcome zone' that brings everyone – staff or visitor – into the office.
Left: At the heart of this project is the desire to blur the boundaries between employee and client space: everything is open and free to view.

Opposite: This open-plan zone is lined with trade literature, which staff can easily access.

When the production company PostPanic moved to its new offices in Amsterdam, it required a workspace that functioned well and engendered a sense of inspiration and creativity. As PostPanic choose to produce, direct, design and animate projects themselves, each of the departments must have clearly defined areas. But at the same time, the brief called for openness and transparency. The design also had to take into account the fact that the workforce fluctuates between fourteen and forty people, depending on the workload.

Architect Maurice Mentjens worked with the existing structure, with its concrete columns, to define the dimensions of the different working areas. The distance between two columns defines the width of the production room, meeting room and staff room. The studio on the mezzanine level above is twice this size.

The tall hall on the ground floor is a neutral space, used as a backdrop for seminars and screenings. An oak grandstand, above which an installation of fluorescent tubes radiates out over the office, doubles as a staircase leading to the mezzanine. A white-tiled bar, intended to resemble an old-fashioned kitchen, is equipped with a grand table for reading and dining. These spaces make up the office recreation area. Wooden beams strung between two columns in the kitchen serve as both a bookcase and a boundary separating the recreation area from the adjacent production room. Floor and walls here are covered with red carpet – a cheap alternative to traditional soundproofing.

Carpet is also used on the floor, walls and table in the meeting room, suggesting a futuristic, cave-like atmosphere; while the mirrored walls of the editing room make the space appear never-ending. Between the two rooms runs a corridor, with a mirrored wall at one end, which again plays with the viewer's sense of space and proportion. On the first floor the oak surface of the grandstand extends along the length of the landing, and a balustrade continues the full width of the floor, connecting the different areas.

Each area of the office has its own atmosphere. In the design studio there are three large tables, each containing eight workstations. To create a distinctive sense of quiet and calm in this room, the floors, walls and balustrade are painted the same shade of green.

The wildly fluctuating number of workers in the office makes storage a critical aspect of the design. In the staff room a tall, square desk provides storage space in the legs.

POSTPANIC OFFICE

Architect: **Maurice Mentjens Design**
Client: **PostPanic**
Location: **Amsterdam, the Netherlands**
Completed: **March 2009**
Size: **570 sq m (6,080 sq ft)**
Budget: **undisclosed**

For maximum flexibility, trolleys are used to store staff belongings and to carry computers; the trolleys can be parked in an open cupboard that extends to the height of the balustrade on the first floor. Here, as well, a visitors' lounge can be created by bringing in two mobile armchairs.

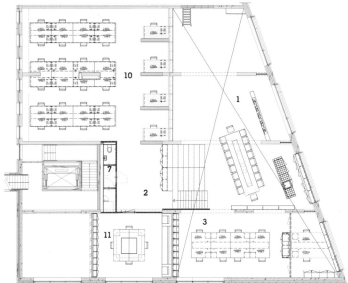

first floor

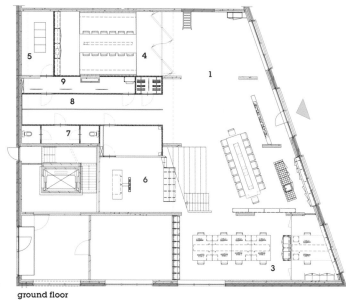

ground floor

1 entrance	7 bathroom
2 stairs/tribune	8 corridor
3 production area	9 storage
4 meeting room	10 2D/3D studio
5 server	11 office
6 edit room	

Page 162: The ground floor of this bright, open environment features an installation of fluorescent tubes on the ceiling.

Left: In an eccentric touch, carpet is applied to the walls as well as the floors, creating an unusual textural effect.
Above: The brief asked that the space have clearly defined areas – such as the design studio and the meeting rooms – but at the same time maintain a sense of openness. This was achieved through keeping internal walls to a minimum and the clever placing of large pieces of furniture.

Opposite: The ground-floor space was conceived as a backdrop for the client's many meetings and seminars. The stairs lead up to a mezzanine level.

Above: The design studio has long green tables, the same shade as the floor, to generate a sense of serenity and calm.
Right: Exposed ductwork imparts an industrial air to the workspace. The desking is flexible so that it can be reconfigured to accommodate fluctuating numbers of staff.

Page 168: The entrance to the meeting room recalls curvy 1960s retro.

Page 169: Because of its low lighting and dark ceiling, the interior of the meeting room has a womb-like quality.

There are not many offices that can boast their own indoor skateboarding bowl, but the Milan store dedicated to Comvert's 'bastard' brand of skate- and snowboarding products is one. Comvert, formed in 1994, wanted to keep in close touch with its target audience of young boarders, and so built the bowl alongside their retail outlet, design studio and their products depot.

The bowl, which is suspended 6 m above the products depot, takes up 200 sq m of space and cost around €100,000. Given the expenditure on this facility, it is no surprise that elsewhere the architects have employed a light touch: they made great use of wood and steel and avoided altering the outer shell of the building.

Previously, the space was known as the Cinema Istria. It was constructed in 1940 and before being converted into an office, was a car dealership. The building has an overall volume of 6,600 cubic metres, and contains an old cinema pit and a suspended balcony. Reinforced-concrete arches make up the roof of the building, and the ceiling lighting was suspended under the vault.

In the new design, the administrative department is situated on the ground floor. The department's desks are located on a larch platform, which levels out the original marble floor and contains the electrical installations. Three banisters help to screen the staff from the view of the store's customers.

The 15-metre-tall products depot in the old cinema pit is simply painted black, while the design studio has been built on the stepped surface of the balcony, using a steel structure attached to the existing concrete beams to support the wooden platform.

In the main entrance of the shop, the cashiers' desks and the clothes displays utilize wood left over from the construction of the offices, and the fitting rooms are made from surplus materials from the bowl.

It was important that all employees connect with each other. This manifests itself not only in their being united in one building, but also in the visibility afforded to different departments through the creation of an open-plan space. The shop floor is visible from the design area, and the designers are not given designated workstations, but rather encouraged to hotdesk. All employees work one month on rotation in the shop to keep them in touch with their customers.

The lower steps of the balcony have been left unmodified, and the original wooden floor and banisters have been restored. This area is used as showroom space, for screenings of skate films, or simply for chilling out, and the existing levels offer maximum flexibility and visibility for whatever activities are going on there.

BASTARD STORE

Architect: **studiometrico**
Client: **Comvert**
Location: **Milan, Italy**
Completed: **October 2008**
Floor space: **1,300 sq m (13,990 sq ft)**
Budget: **€2 million**

Page 170: The administration department is located on the ground floor, where the original, patterned terrazzo flooring from the cinema has been kept and gives the office character.

Opposite: The indoor skate bowl attracts skateboarders from far and wide who want to test their skills (*top left*). It was constructed in a space that has housed a cinema and subsequently a car showroom (*top right and bottom left*). The idea behind the design was to attract skateboarding fans to the 'bastard' complex, where, because the staff work rotational shifts in the retail outlet, a connection with customers is maintained (*bottom right*).

Right: Through its sheer scale the elevated skateboarding bowl dominates the project. Opposite the skate bowl, on a slope, are the design studio and the showroom. **Below:** The old cinema pit, which remains from the building's former use, now houses the products depot.

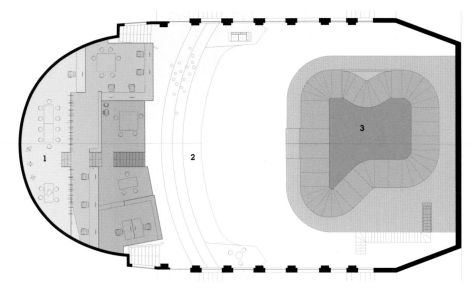

upper level

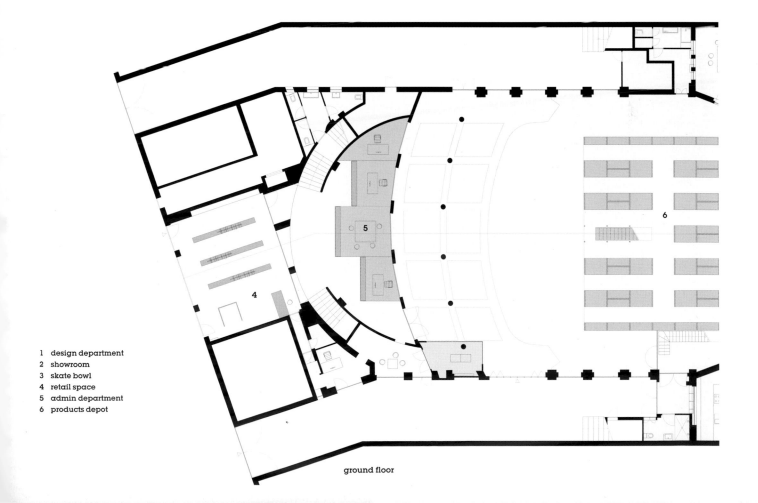

1   design department
2   showroom
3   skate bowl
4   retail space
5   admin department
6   products depot

ground floor

Opposite: This project is not only an office, but also the 'bastard' skateboarding label's retail outlet and an events space.

Above left: The design team do not have their own desks, instead they hotdesk each day when they come into the office.
Above right: The skateboarding bowl is visible from the design studio, so that the designers stay in constant touch with their market. **Left:** A larch platform high in the building provides the workspace for the designers – a link to the ground floor, where the administration department's workstations also sit on a larch platform.

Marketing and communications agency Billington Cartmell wanted its offices in Fulham, West London, to take a stand against the trend within media workspaces to focus on expensive materials such as poured resin, Corian and acres of space filled with designer furniture. According to the agency head, Ian Billington, the focus should be on highly skilled staff delivering excellent service to the client, rather than on lavish fittings and furnishings for the sake of ostentation. Therefore, the budget was closely monitored.

The building was initially conceived by CZWG architects and the interior designed by Platform group, who worked on it in three phases. Known as the Blue Building, the office makes use of skylights to bring natural light deep into the plan.

The main workspace, on the third floor of the Blue Building, has been kept as unadorned as possible: the galvanized, raised floor left was naked to create an industrial feel. To comply with the cost-conscious approach, storage cabinets, desk and meeting tables were all sourced from Ikea. This back-to-basics was, however, always accompanied by a sense of fun. A vinyl runway delineates the main circulation routes for the building, and is inset with images from iconic video games such as Pac Man and Space Invaders. At the far end of the space, the floor-to-ceiling glass wall is screen-printed to look like bookshelves, giving it a mock stately home aesthetic. The office even has a secret door leading to a meeting area, which is styled as a billiard room.

The reception is one of the newest parts of the scheme. The brief here was to enliven a dull, lifeless area and to provide better sight lines while utilizing the new Billington Cartmell brand colours of black and green. One wall is an abstracted barcode, made of Reno Bond – a lightweight yet rigid material more commonly used in signage. A padded and buttoned white leather-effect panel incorporates concealed lighting, which accents the brand identity by highlighting the company name. One of the buttons on the reception desk echoes this theme. The straightjacket-like magazine rack at one end references the old adage 'You don't have to be mad to work here...'

The boardroom, also recently renovated, subtly alludes to James Bond. The striking environment offers many talking points, without descending to gimmickry: a glass-topped meeting table features an aerial view of the locale, in which the Blue Building figures prominently; the curtains are edged in dinner-jacket silk with cummerbund tiebacks; and the lamp bases are made out of revolvers. Although there are some high-end pieces here – the Arper chairs and the Flos lights – the overall effect strongly projects the 'no nonsense' work ethic of the client.

BILLINGTON CARTMELL OFFICE

Architect: **Platform group**
Client: **Billington Cartmell**
Location: **London, UK**
Completed: **2008**
Size: **1,360 sq m (14,590 sq ft)**
Budget: **undisclosed**

Page 176: In one of the office meeting rooms the tabletop is imprinted with aerial photography images of the company's West London environs.

Left: The reception area features a buttoned, padded surface on the wall and on the desk, and the clear branding gives a confident first impression to anyone entering the workplace. Below: Break-out space forms an important part of the working environment for this advertising agency.

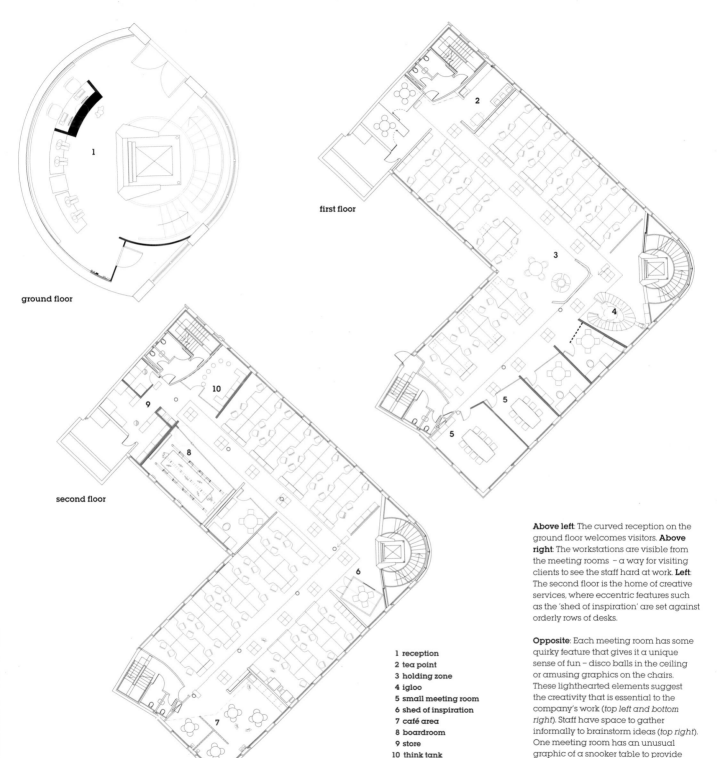

ground floor

first floor

second floor

1 reception
2 tea point
3 holding zone
4 igloo
5 small meeting room
6 shed of inspiration
7 café area
8 boardroom
9 store
10 think tank

Above left: The curved reception on the ground floor welcomes visitors. **Above right**: The workstations are visible from the meeting rooms – a way for visiting clients to see the staff hard at work. **Left**: The second floor is the home of creative services, where eccentric features such as the 'shed of inspiration' are set against orderly rows of desks.

Opposite: Each meeting room has some quirky feature that gives it a unique sense of fun – disco balls in the ceiling or amusing graphics on the chairs. These lighthearted elements suggest the creativity that is essential to the company's work (*top left and bottom right*). Staff have space to gather informally to brainstorm ideas (*top right*). One meeting room has an unusual graphic of a snooker table to provide clients with a lasting memory of their visit to the agency (*bottom left*).

The Harmonia 57 project takes living architecture to a new level. It is located in Harmonia Street, an artistic community on the west side of São Paulo, where there are many galleries. The graffiti in the alley in front of the building gives the viewer a clue to the area's left-field kudos. To make the building 'live' Triptyque decided to cover the thick walls with a layer of vegetation that acts as a skin to the structure. The density of the organic concrete has allowed several plant species to grow successfully, and eventually the vegetation will cover the building.

Water is an integral part of how this workspace functions. The project is situated in a challenging location that is prone to flooding. The project itself is its own ecosystem: rainwater and water from the soil are drained, treated and reused. The pipes that serve the whole building, as well as the pumps, sprinklers and water-treatment system, cover the exterior walls like blood vessels in the body. Some of these 'veins and arteries' also form guard rails.

It seems as if the project has been designed inside out: the exposed nature of the pipework contrasts with a slick, minimalist interior. The grey of the exterior concrete is much more roughly hewn than the interior, which has a luminous quality.

The layout of the space is simple yet noteworthy. A metallic footbridge connects the two large blocks that make up Harmonia 57. In the middle of the two blocks an internal plaza has been created to encourage chance encounters between the local creatives who work in the offices.

In the front block, the windows cut into the concrete are designed to be 'eyes' so that staff can look out over the city. At the same time the feature creates visual interest when viewed from various points. A giant concrete 'mouth' seems to consume the cars parked in front of the building. The block at the back is solid, apart from a birdcage-like structure on top. The differences between the two blocks create an interesting proportional interplay. This visual playfulness is echoed by the terraces on each floor, which alter the light available in the internal spaces and the transparency to the outside world.

The building, like all living things, will change through time as it breathes and functions. The plants will grow – thanks to the rain and the irrigation system – and the walls will weather naturally, a process that will produce different forms and colours.

HARMONIA 57

Architect: **Triptyque**
Client: **IV Incorporadora**
Location: **São Paulo, Brazil**
Completed: **2008**
Size: **1,100 sq m (11,840 sq ft)**
Budget: **€300 million**

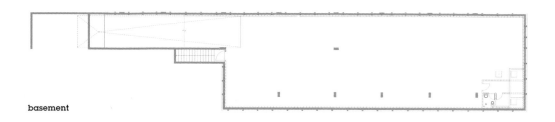

basement

ground floor

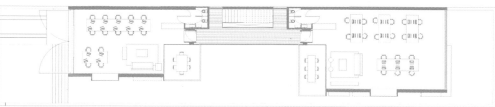

first floor

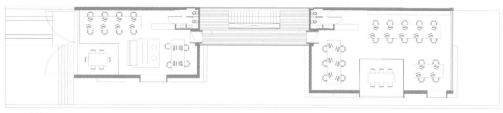

second floor

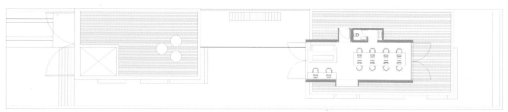

third floor

Page 182: The office is located in an up-and-coming part of São Paulo.

This page: Harmonia 57 is made up of two blocks, connected via simple metal footbridges on the first and second floors. Designed to encourage movement around the building, the bridges create opportunities for chance meetings between staff.

Opposite: The walls of the building are covered in vegetation: several species at once can grow here, providing the office with its own living ecosystem.

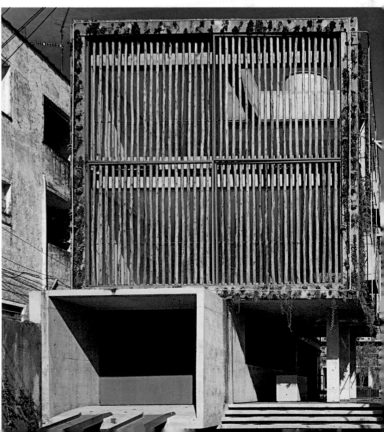

LARGE

(Over 2,200 sq m)

The HafenCity in Hamburg is an ongoing urban development programme to revive a stretch of land by the river Elbe's waterfront with a mixture of offices, residential and retail builds. One of the first completed offices is Unilever's new HQ, which stands on the edge of the water like a ship about to head out to sea. Inspired by the maritime context, Behnisch Architekten have created a modern workplace that feels like a cruise ship. The sloping roof structure looks like a sail, while the stairs with their slim balustrades are reminiscent of a ferry. These stairs, along with bridges and ramps and a mix of indoor and outdoor balconies, connect the various levels to encourage movement throughout the building, echoing the client's work philosophy: there is more than one way that leads to the goal.

Bright orange, yellow and green light up the interior. On a sunny day, when the sun shines through the central atrium's glass roof, you almost feel as if you are on holiday in the office. Natural daylight floods the building. It is supplemented by a newly developed LED illumination system, SMD LED, especially impressive in the suspended light circles that double as an art installation. These lights are 70% more efficient than halogen or conventional bulbs.

The whole project is built on the basic principles of sustainable architecture: the ecological balance of each material was checked to ensure that it was free from volatile solvents, biocides or halogen. Tropical hardwoods are from certified sustainable sources.

From an architectural point of view, the exterior's double façade is an innovative accomplishment. The largest membrane structure of its kind to date, the single ETFE (Ethylene Tetrafluoroethylene) polymer construction wraps around the building like a second skin. The more common cushion-form ETFE is replaced here with a single system that ensures transparency so as not to block the spectacular harbour views. The tautly fixed foil protects the glass façade like an airy parasol, shielding the building from strong sea winds, while also shading it from the sun. The structure is much lighter than a standard glazing solution. The ETFE is stretched over individual frames, which, when combined with the free flow of air between the two claddings, means it does not need compartmentalization for fire safety. This single membrane construction has a slightly angular 'saddle' form: the load is carried along both vertical and

UNILEVER HEADQUARTERS

Architect/Design: **Behnisch Architekten**
Client: **Hochtief for Unilever HQ**
Location: **HafenCity, Hamburg, Germany**
Completed: **September 2009**
Size: **20,000 sq m (215,280 sq ft)**
Budget: **undisclosed**

horizontal sides of the membrane sheet, and wind suction cables take the pressure off the membrane at the bottom. What makes the façade so special is that it has individually controllable windows and sunshades. Each employee can also manually regulate the radiators to achieve an ideal personal temperature.

The inclusive character of the office represents a very novel approach to office design. Behnisch created an atrium that is open to the public during office hours. There are no workspaces on the ground floor; instead there is a spa, a shop selling Unilever products, and a restaurant with a stunning outdoor terrace offering breathtaking harbour views. The 'eat and meet' concept continues on the staff-only floors, where there are no allocated workstations, but rather a variety of seating arrangements to allow employees to work anywhere. The Unilever office is a perfect example of how a setting can inspire pioneering designs.

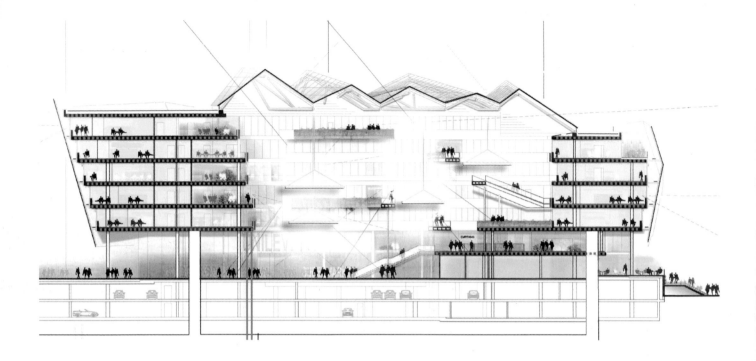

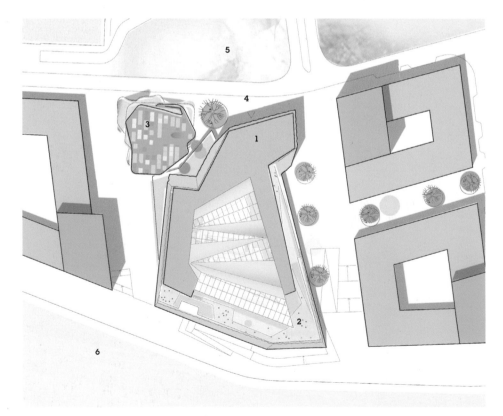

1 main office
2 terrace
3 Marco Polo Tower
4 main entrance north
5 Marco Polo Terrace
6 river Elbe

Page 190: The grand façade, made from ETFE, is transparent so as not to obstruct the fabulous harbour views.

Left and above: The building was designed to fit an odd-shaped site and to correlate with the immediate architectural environment, as shown in the master plan.

Opposite: The ETFE cladding has been uniquely developed to deal with the extreme weather conditions of the North Sea front. The outside terrace is open to the public, who take full advantage of its recreational possibilities.

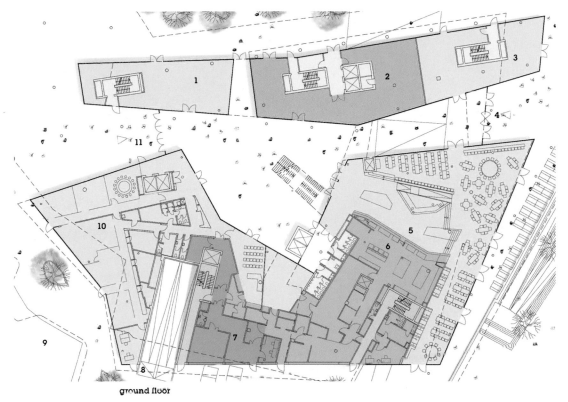

ground floor

1 spa
2 supermarket
3 café
4 main entrance south
5 staff canteen
6 kitchen
7 deliveries
8 entrance to underground car park
9 Marco Polo Tower
10 test kitchen
11 main entrance north
12 open-plan workspace
13 meeting point

third floor

Above: On the ground floor the building is shared by public facilities, such as a shop, a spa and a restaurant. An outdoor sun terrace provides a place to relax and view the harbour.
Left: The staff-only top floor houses open-plan workspace, which is arranged around the atrium. A skylight in the centre of the roof lets daylight reach the whole building.

Opposite: The light rings use a newly developed SMD LED system that is 70% more energy efficient than halogen bulbs.

This page and opposite: The inside of the Unilever office is dominated by steel beams and light features. The seating clusters, overlooking the foyer in areas that have the feel of interior balconies, encourage impromptu meetings. The bright natural daylight and the waterfront views create a sense of holiday.

Converting redundant buildings into offices can be a very resourceful way of transforming existing spaces, and when the building to be transformed is a local landmark, it adds character to the refurbishments in a way that makes the new space particularly distinctive. In Buchs, Switzerland, an iconic feed mill had been towering above the otherwise low-rise buildings since the 1950s. KaundBe architects wanted to salvage the recognizable structure and give it a new lease of life as an office block, keeping the dimensions of the former industrial space.

The mill is located near train tracks so that its products could be easily transported. On the other side of the site is a dense residential area characterized by small houses. The architects wanted to create a façade that would form a bridge between the smaller silhouettes of the neighbouring houses and the comparatively huge volume of the high-rise mill. They achieved this unification through a simple design composed of two different window formats arranged in a seemingly random configuration over the mill's new surface. Dark-blue sheet-metal frames accentuate the windows and make them protrude from the façade like piercing eyes gazing into the distance. These 'eyes' also draw attention away from the dominance of the tall, vertical tower.

The floor plan is divided into two main sections: the tower block and the lower mill building. The tower houses a new entrance, lifts, bathrooms, and offices that go up eight floors and have impressive views. The lower building only rises four storeys, but offers large, open-plan spaces free from supporting columns. Both the tower and the main building have small terraces that provide outdoor space.

KaundBe's choice of materials was inspired by colours and styles found in industrial manufacturing plants. The façade, clad in grey metal sheets, creates a factoryesque backdrop for the remarkable blue windows. The existing structure of the mill was reinforced with concrete, resulting in a compact, engineered edifice. The interior design of the building clearly reflects the industrial past of the mill; exposed concrete surfaces were left untreated to maintain the raw feel of the space and walls and ceilings impress visitors with their size and height. A distinct colour concept highlights the various parts of the office, with the bright blue of the window frames echoed in the interior on all of the walls. Technical installations in the ceiling are not covered over but left visible, which allows for easy access and saves on cost, but also complements the building's industrial aesthetic.

Transformation of the mill into a workplace has the economic advantage of a substantially higher area utilization ratio, and at the same time offers offices with impressive views of the Rhine Valley. In comparison to demolition fees and all of the costs involved, the refurbishment of the existing structure is cost effective. The mostly untreated interior finish and the simple colour concept also kept costs low. The mill's new façade, with its unique arrangement of windows, has modernized a derelict building and its urban surrounding all at once.

DIE FUTTERMÜHLE

Architect: **KaundBe Architekten**
Client: **Lorigenhof**
Location: **Buchs, Switzerland**
Completed: **Autumn 2008**
Size: **2,330 sq m (25,000 sq ft)**
Budget: **€3.75 million**

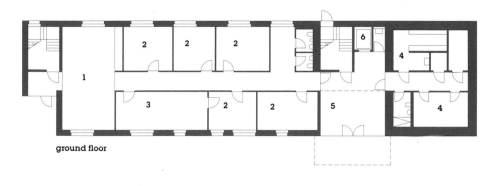

ground floor

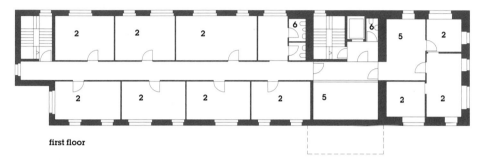

first floor

1 break room
2 office
3 conference room
4 services
5 lobby
6 facilities
7 roof deck

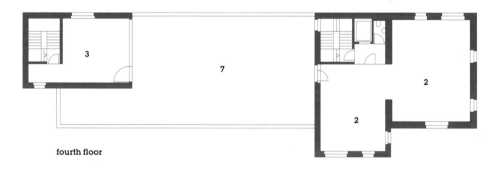

fourth floor

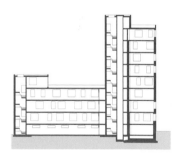

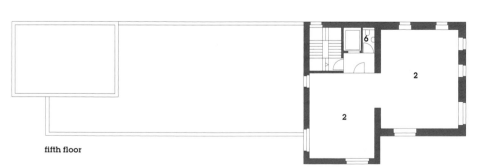

fifth floor

Page 198: The positioning of the windows and their unusual proportions give this refurbished factory an unconventional character in a conservative setting.

Above: The main horizontal arm of the building anchors the tower. **Left**: The roof of the horizontal arm provides an outdoor terrace, which is accessible from the fourth floor of the tower.

Opposite: Pictures of the old building and its refurbished form show how the classic rectangular design was reinterpreted as a contemporary tower block.

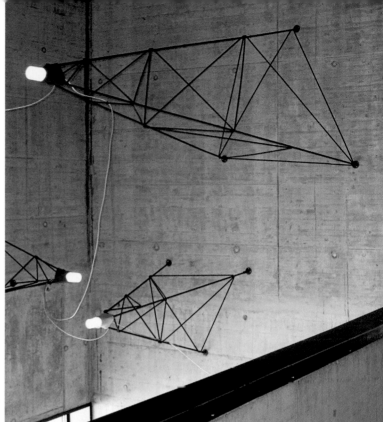

Pages 202–03: Inside, a raw, industrial ethos harks back to the building's origins as a mill.

This page and opposite: The use of basic furnishings and light fixtures contributed considerably to controlling the cost of the refurbishment. The interior finish uses largely untreated materials and the colour concept is simple.

No office design book would be complete without a project from Clive Wilkinson Architects, the California-based design practice that has pioneered creative workplace design for years. No surprise then that JWT, formerly J. Walter Thompson, one of the oldest advertising agencies in the world, called on Clive Wilkinson's expertise to transform both their office and their entire corporate culture. The brightly coloured fit-out may look like a playground, but the concept behind this open space is geared towards a physical, behavioural and virtual transformation that could not have been achieved without a new, progressive and democratic layout.

Wilkinson's design concept is based on the idea of a tree as a metaphor for storytelling. The inspiration came from JWT's shift from projecting messages to the consumer to creating experiences, which reward the public's time and attention. The architects picked up on the storytelling aspect of this new method of JWT's engagement with customers and turned it into the thematic thread for the whole workplace. The tree narrative begins with a main 'trunk', which houses the atrium and a staircase connecting all of the floors. The 'branches' spread outwards and contain numerous meeting rooms, which take the form of green cone-shaped larger spaces or circular structures that use fabric padding to create smaller tent-like spaces. Each of the sixteen different tents is linked to a familiar story or book, and the designers have decorated them by cutting the first line of that story out of the tent fabric using a CNC machine. The cut-out letters hang down like leaves on a tree, creating windows into the meeting pods, and casting interesting shadows.

Fabrics were chosen for their ecological qualities in addition to their tactile features, and sustainably harvested red oak throughout keeps in line with the 'tree' theme. A lot of time was spent on specifying the right furniture to offer both a good price point and valid green credentials. The atrium was carved out of an existing floor plate and the pre-cast concrete treads were used for the staircase to keep costs under control. Yet the architects managed to use these cost-saving features in a creative way. Similarly the elevator lobbies have metal mesh ceilings that sparkle in the lighting. This dramatic feature, however, is simply due to an expanded metal mesh panel and a t-bar grid.

JWT OFFICE

Architect: **Clive Wilkinson Architects**
Client: **JWT**
Location: **New York, USA**
Completed: **February 2008**
Size: **23,230 sq m (250,000 sq ft)**
Budget: **undisclosed**

Bold colours and fabrics function as intuitive navigating devices throughout the entire office space. The vibrant colour scheme ties the whole office together, and the floor plan is based on a circulation scheme to promote movement through the space. Mezzanine floors were introduced to connect all of the levels vertically. The space is divided into hot and cold zones: hot zones are public spaces with high interaction, like the cafés, and cold zones focus on private areas for high concentration work, such as the library. The idea is that staff are not confined to working at desks, but can make use of a larger area – they are spoilt for choice with the number of options available to them. 'Un-programmed' spaces aim to get employees to determine their individual work patterns. According to the client, the business is already running more efficiently with the new space's dynamics of mobility, interaction and collaboration, and the office has successfully brought this traditional advertising agency into the new media age.

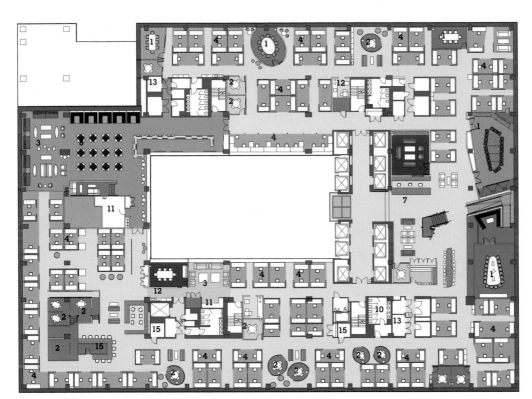

second floor

1 conference room
2 small meeting room
3 lounge
4 open workstations
5 office
6 lift lobby
7 reception
8 town hall/café
9 bar
10 bathrooms
11 pantry
12 copy/print
13 services/systems
14 post room
15 storage
16 AV production
17 IT

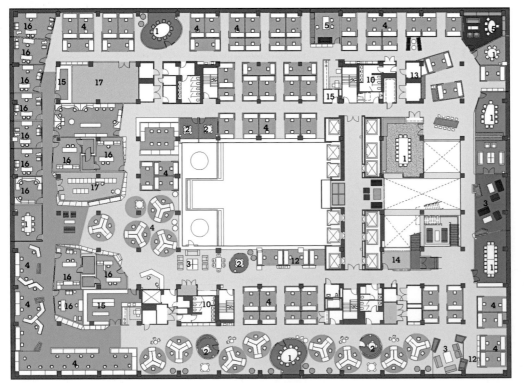

third floor

Page 206: The floors of this ad agency are interconnected spatially and integrated through their decor. The effect is to create an open, transparent space.

This page: The detailed plans show how diverse the working scenarios are on each floor: little clusters spread out across the floors, making ingenious use of the space.

Opposite: By means of mezzanine floors (*top left*), a library (*top right*), designer lamps (*bottom left*) and wallpapered surfaces set against glass-box meeting rooms (*bottom right*) Clive Wilkinson focused on creating a balance of formal and casual communal areas and private client areas.

Pages 210–11: The openness of this building is based on a democratic layout, a concept developed by the architect in response to the company's view of its contemporary work model.

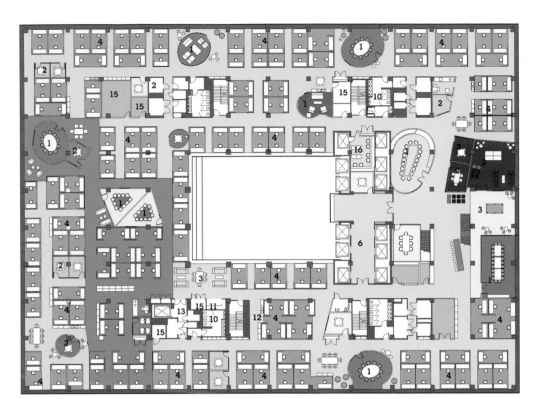

fourth floor

1 conference room
2 small meeting room
3 lounge
4 open workstations
5 office
6 lift lobby
7 reception
8 town hall/café
9 bar
10 bathrooms
11 pantry
12 copy/print
13 services/systems
14 post room
15 storage
16 AV production
17 IT

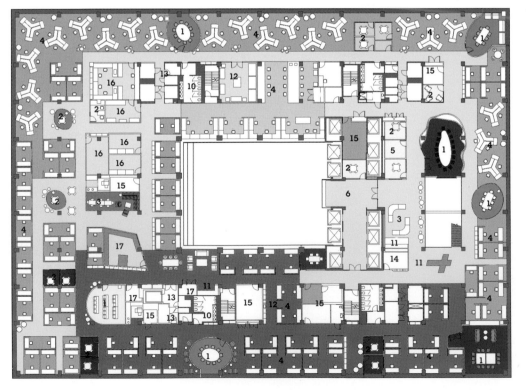

fifth floor

This page: Working clusters of four to eight people are grouped round the central space on every floor. Common to all floors is an open format, offering a mix of lounge and meeting spaces, with flexible work arrangements.

Opposite: A selection of quotations and phrases from books and poems have been computer-cut into the fabric that lines some of the meeting-room walls; sometimes the letters are peeled back from the surface, producing an intriguing positive/negative effect.

Pages 214–15: To create this generous double-height space, floor slabs between the first and second floors, and the third and fourth floors, were cut away. The atrium of the entrance hall is now ten metres high, with a concrete staircase rising through it.

brothers
grimm

The new working facilities for the Department of Biochemistry at Oxford are set to revolutionize the way its 300 researchers and post-graduate students work. Hawkins\Brown pursued a 'new working methodology' that had effective space management at the heart of its design. The workplace breaks the past cycle of refurnishing every eighteen months when a new research team comes in, as the new fully flexible and adaptable space accommodates change without the need for 'stripping out'. For instance, the bench length per scientist can be regulated, allowing the modules in the general laboratories to accommodate a range of twenty-four to thirty people.

The cost-saving implications are apparent. As with the so-called 'activity-based research organization' approach, Hawkins\Brown eradicated the duplication of support facilities so common in academic, grant-funded research spaces. Previously these facilities were arranged by topics, but to economize the required space the new workspace groups together researchers from different scientific disciplines who perform similar activities. On the whole, the new building aims to implement an ethos of interdisciplinary working, and the potential of cross-fertilization is brought to life in this research hub. This is particularly pioneering given the nature of lab work. The high level of transparency, with laboratories visible even from outside the building, promotes a large collaborative setting for the scientists.

In addition to making the workflow more efficient, the building ticks all the boxes regarding environmental accountability. All of the interior workspaces revolve around an expansive 400 sq metre timber-clad atrium that is naturally ventilated. The height of the space allows fresh air to be drawn in at basement level, and then run through a large duct and eventually extracted through the chimneys on the roof. Photovoltaic cells are integrated into the glazed roof lights, providing energy as well as shading to prevent overheating. Even the toilets are flushed using water from a rainwater-harvesting installation on the roof.

While such features are not cheap, their longevity makes this workplace a modern prototype of economical architecture. And the focus on creating positive spaces outside the building to promote a pedestrian-friendly environment echoes architect Frank Duffy's vision for twenty-first-century offices to emphasize the importance of interstitial space.

DEPARTMENT OF BIOCHEMISTRY, UNIVERSITY OF OXFORD

Architect: **Hawkins\Brown**
Client: **University of Oxford**
Location: **Oxford, UK**
Completed: **October 2008**
Size: **12,000 sq m (129,170 sq ft)**
Budget: **£49 million**

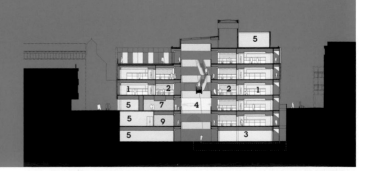

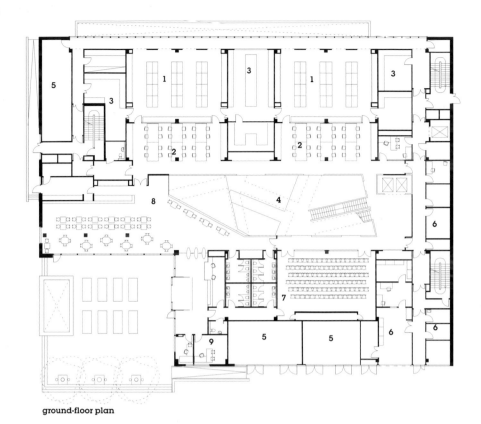

ground-floor plan

1 main laboratory
2 write up space
3 support/specialist laboratory
4 atrium
5 plant
6 ancillary space
7 seminar/meeting room
8 café
9 offices

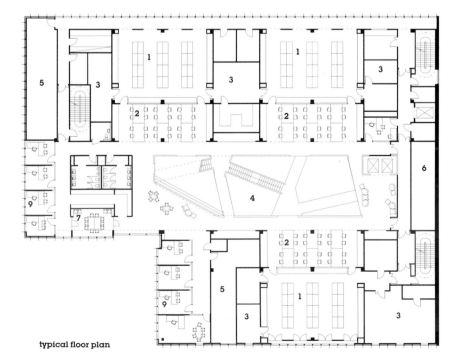

typical floor plan

Page 216: Glass artworks adorn the windows of the new biochemistry department in the University of Oxford, which won a RIBA award in 2009 for its contribution to British architecture.

Page 217: Two floors of the building are underground; the lower one houses a specialist laboratory.

This page: The traditionally closed environment of research labs has been broken down into a modern office floor plan, with a variety of different types of work zone.

Opposite: Laboratories, meeting rooms, areas for concentrated work and auditoriums are mixed in the open and light environment of the new department building.

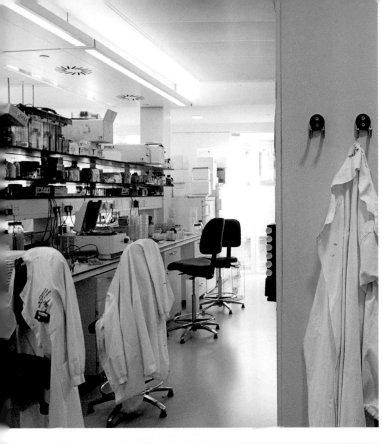

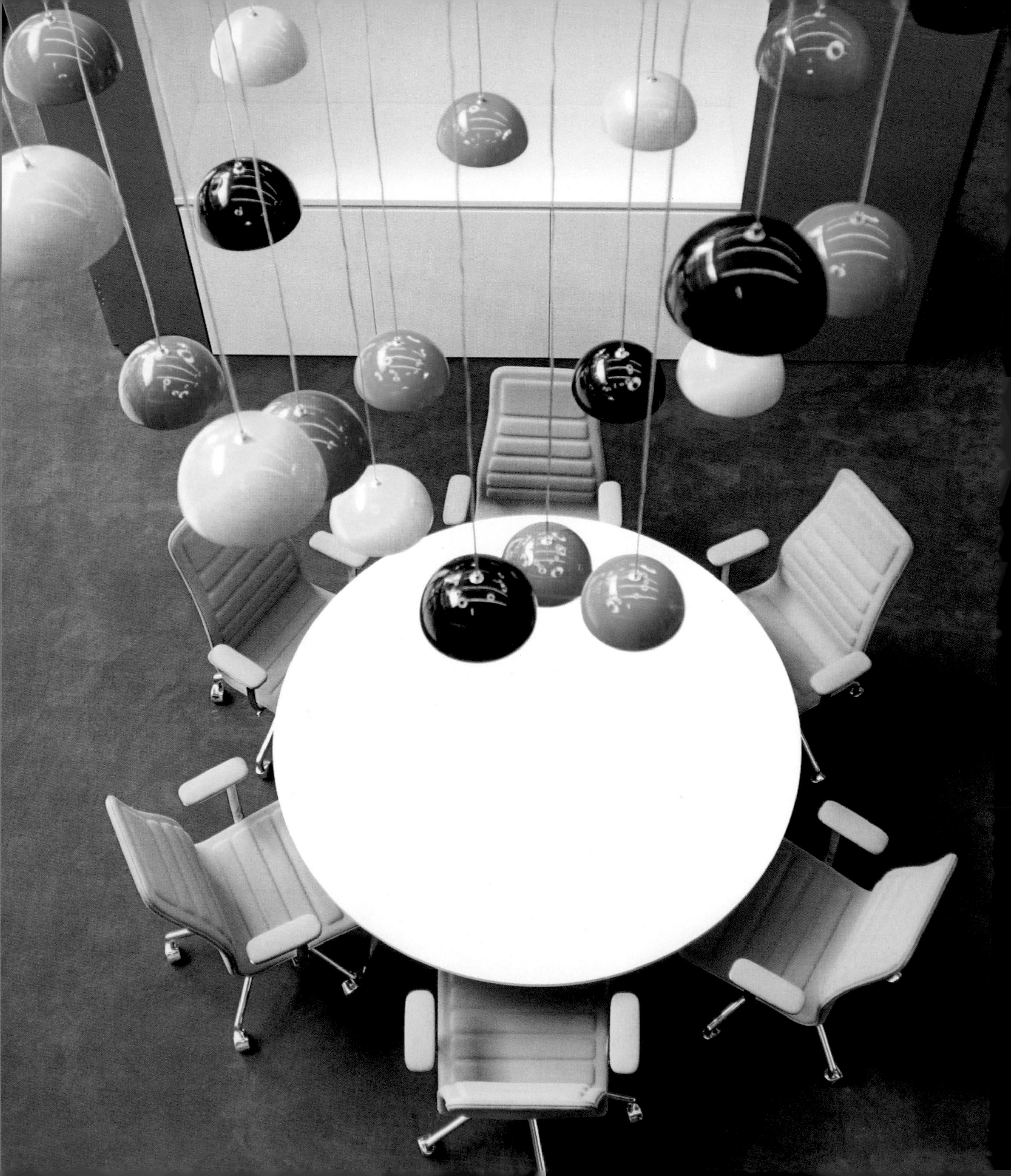

Microsoft offices, like most blue chip workplaces, aim to become living examples of how their products work. This idea is definitely evident in the company's Dutch headquarters, which have set a benchmark for how technology can optimize working procedures. The new office fit-out, designed by London-based design practice SevilPeach, brings popular phrases from workplace strategists such as 'non-territorial' and 'activity-based' working to life. No employee, not even executives and senior management, has a desk. In fact, the management policy goes so far as to encourage staff not to come to the office, but work from wherever suits them best. After all, Microsoft creates the technology that allows flexible working, so why retain the archaic mentality derived from the late nineteenth-century ideas of efficiency management guru F. W. Taylor that the definition of working is staff sitting at their desks?

This shift in working style did create a new challenge for the designer, however. If employees no longer have to come to the physical office to work, there is a 'physical minimum' that affects the design brief: less furniture, less paper, fewer people. SevilPeach intelligently created a variety of spaces across the floor that can accommodate up to 1,000 employees if needed. The central staircase is the social heart of the building, creating a vertical and horizontal connection across the six floors. The open space is essentially broken down into many mini environments spread throughout the office, and the architects used textured panels as dividers to control acoustics and soften the space. Clusters of different seating arrangements, meeting rooms, work carousels, relaxation zones, cafés, sleeping pods and outdoor facilities, all furnished with a range of different tables and chairs, emancipate the worker by providing lots of choice.

Post-occupancy studies show that the scheme has worked. Staff are actually spending more time working in the social areas, such as the café and food corner, than at the typical office workstation-style booths. This shows that the social nature of humans remains the key *raison d'être* for offices, and that despite modern technology, employees prefer to work with other people around them. At the same time, the possibility of working in settings such as coffee shops, like Starbucks, has influenced workplace design to emulate 'urban settings' as staff seek similar set-ups to feel comfortable at work. The office has become a live case study for the effectiveness of a 'no-desk-allocation' scheme and, consequently, will influence the development of Microsoft's computer programs in the future.

MICROSOFT DUTCH HEADQUARTERS

Architect: **SevilPeach**
Client: **Microsoft**
Location: **Amsterdam, the Netherlands**
Completed: **August 2008**
Size: **10,890 sq m (117,220 sq ft)**
Budget: **undisclosed**

Page 220: Designer furniture, lamps and accessories introduce colour into this huge space.

This page: The options for working scenarios in this office are unprecedented. There are no allocated workstations or rows of desks. Instead, emulating an urban landscape, each floor provides a mixture of spaces to work in: the first floor (*below*), a social hub, contains a diverse mixture of areas, including sleep pods, a think tank, and even cabins in the central courtyard for meetings. Diagonal walls create a dynamic flow.

Opposite: The Dutch headquarters of Microsoft represent a radical implementation of non-territorial working: no member of staff has a permanent desk, not even the executives. A range of seating and desks are provided and staff work wherever they like.

1 entrance
2 café
3 auditorium
4 void
5 lift lobby
6 work/eat/meet
7 catering
8 copy
9 relax/sleep pods
10 telephone booth
11 quiet work zones
12 stand-up meeting room
13 boardroom
14 think tank
15 meeting cabins
16 courtyard
17 lockers
18 coffee point
19 meet/work
20 concentration rooms
21 meeting rooms
22 roof

typical office floor

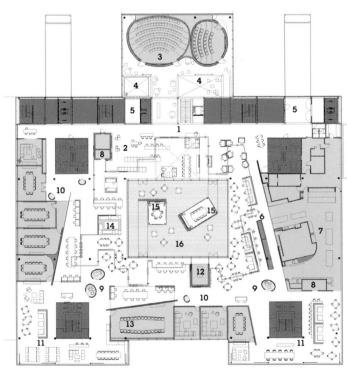

first floor (social hub)

This page and opposite: SevilPeach created a mix of seating options, from upholstered chairs in the lounge areas, to moulded chairs set at long wooden canteen benches or communal tables, and recliners on the outdoor terraces. Post-occupancy studies have shown that staff prefer working in the social areas, such as the café, to using the concentration pods.

Pages 226–27: Microsoft's office is meant to demonstrate that their technology promotes a natural flow of working. SevilPeach believes that people prefer not to sit in the same space all day and welcome the opportunity to move from one area to another, using in turn shared desk space, standing tables, sofas, benches or separate individual working docks.

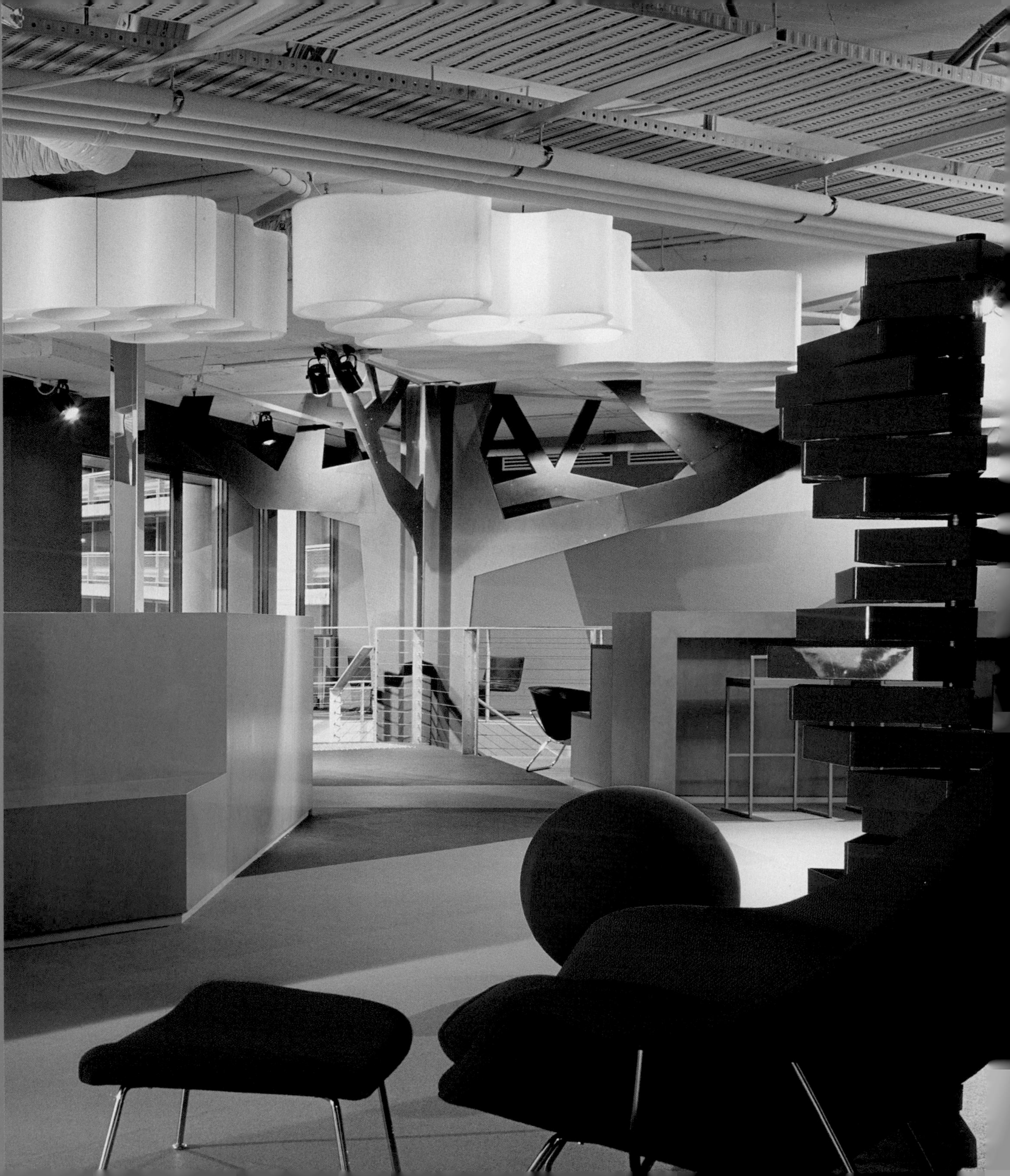

This training environment for the ANZ Bank, on the first floor of its flagship office in Melbourne's Docklands area, is designed as an antidote to the traditional idea of a corporate office in order to stimulate creativity. It forms part of the bank's objective to provide a place for different learning and development activities, as well as formal and informal gatherings and events. The brief called for a design that challenges the perception of a traditional training centre, removing the user from the world of banking while attracting, retaining and developing the best talent.

The training area has over 200 users each day and consists of thirteen learning and break-out rooms, six meeting rooms, plus an outdoor area. It is open from early morning to late at night, so the space needs to be highly flexible and adaptable.

Inspiration was taken from *Alice in Wonderland*, and visitors enter the centre through a door that plays with perspective slightly, making them feel as if they are flying down a rabbit hole to a place they were not expecting.

There is playful use of space and colour in order to create a sense of fun, using materials such as recycled patterned rubber, sustainable plywood and low VOC paints. The rawness and basic detailing of these materials enhance the functionality of the space. The idea behind the centre is that it is intended to sharpen the senses of its users, encouraging them to exceed expectations. Staff climb the 'Tree of Knowledge', around which is a utilitarian, almost scaffold-like, central staircase from ground floor to first floor; at the point where they come across the canopy they begin their journey of discovery.

The theory of learning outside the classroom influenced the planning of the centre. Designers Hassell created intimate nooks between more formal settings. The spaces are supported by technological aids such as interactive walls and podcasting facilities to record and replay training sessions. These are intended to promote memory and learning, and are also used to share information with other parts of the business to support international communication within the bank.

The space is devoid of ANZ's logo, corporate colours or standard office furniture. Instead, it is dominated by shades of green and red, with natural lighting in abundance to create a light, bright interior. Unusual,

ANZ LEARNING CENTRE

Architect: **Hassell**
Client: **ANZ Bank**
Location: **Melbourne, Australia**
Completed: **September 2007**
Size: **3,000 sq m (32,290 sq ft)**
Budget: **undisclosed**

contemporary choices were made for the seating specification in order to enhance the sensory experience of the space and create an invigorating environment.

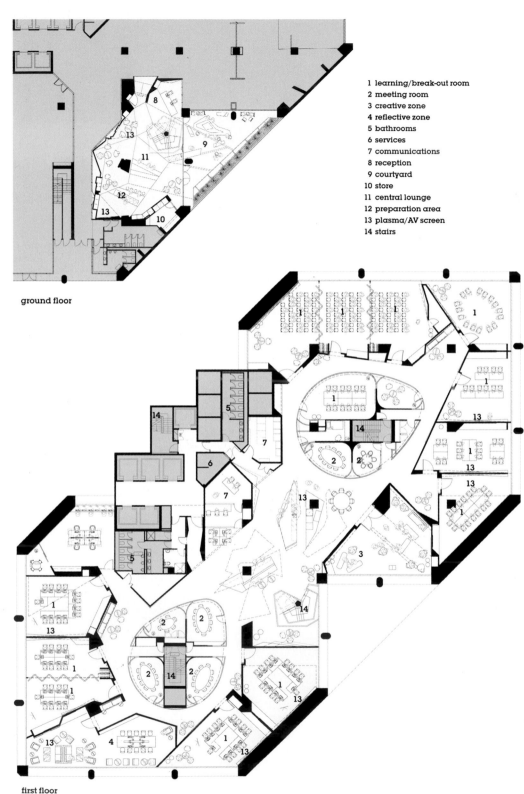

ground floor

1 learning/break-out room
2 meeting room
3 creative zone
4 reflective zone
5 bathrooms
6 services
7 communications
8 reception
9 courtyard
10 store
11 central lounge
12 preparation area
13 plasma/AV screen
14 stairs

Page 228: The 'Tree of Knowledge' is the focal point of this Australian bank's training centre.

Pages 230-31: Staff begin their journey of learning by climbing the stairs beside the 'Tree of Knowledge'.

Above: The ground floor also provides more relaxed settings – the courtyard, for example – combined with hi-tech features to promote different kinds of encounters. **Left**: Meeting, learning and break-out spaces are situated around the perimeter of the building and clustered near to staircases in bubble-like shapes. Around and between these areas there are intimate nooks, which encourage informal interaction.

Opposite: Bright colours, such as the green used here, are important in this office interior as they inject a sense of fun and informality into the surroundings.

Page 234-35: The varied silhouettes of the furniture, like other features of the design, are intended to stimulate the senses and inspire a positive, receptive frame of mind in the users of the office.

first floor

The Arts Council National Office in London has been remodelled for the benefit of 250 staff members who are based there, but also as a resource for the organization's nine regional offices. Architects Caruso St John worked with artists and graphic and media designers to produce a new, appealing workplace in a seven-storey Victorian building on a tight budget. The refurbishment saw previously labyrinthine, partitioned offices with low suspended ceilings transformed into an open environment with an industrial feel. Staff now work in groups at large tables, and the expectation is that over time the offices will mutate into a hotdesking model. Personal storage has therefore been kept to a minimum. On each floor there are freestanding hubs that incorporate storage, kitchen facilities, and booths for private phone calls.

Stripping back the interior to the shell serves the lobby particularly well, effectively doubling its size. Light is brought in from two directions and gives the public a glimpse of what goes on at the Arts Council. The lobby floor is a hardwearing linoleum chequerboard, and Caruso St John also designed the reception desk and wardrobes, which house the fan coil units. Douglas fir ply joinery is used throughout and, though a cost-conscious option, is not one that is detrimental to the aesthetic appeal of the space. The 5-metre floor-to-ceiling height of the space, simply lit with a pendant light, presents the perfect place to show artists' work and promote Arts Council England's function as a vital funding body.

Colour plays an important part in this project and artist Lothar Götz was commissioned to produce a three-dimensional construct within the building. The shell is painted in a range of greys, a different shade for each of the seven storeys. The subtle tonal differences of the walls and ceilings are only really visible from the stairwell.

There is also a more vibrant colour palette to accent the meeting rooms and lift core. Here Götz has used half a dozen colours, the arrangements varying from floor to floor to create visual interest and an abstract, spring-garden-like feel. The effect is most striking in the meeting rooms on the lowest two floors, where added playfulness comes courtesy of upturned lightboxes, which are recessed into suspended aluminium plates. In the private phone booths a more intense colour is used on the interior than on the outside to give a jewelry-box feel. Where there are many roughly hewn or exposed elements, colour both communicates the spirit of the building and engages the response of those who work and visit there.

ARTS COUNCIL NATIONAL OFFICE

Architect: **Caruso St John**
Client: **Arts Council England**
Location: **London, UK**
Completed: **2008**
Size: **3,300 sq m (35,520 sq ft)**
Budget: **£3 million**

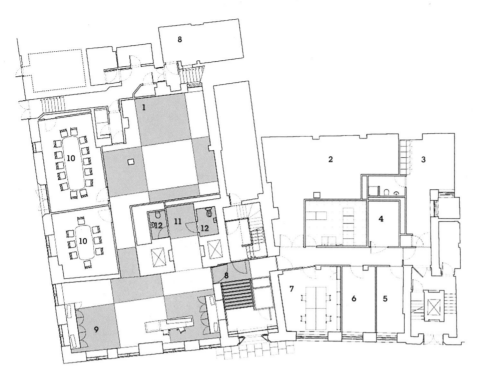

lower ground floor

1 canteen
2 back of house
3 bike store
4 back of house
5 post room
6 printing
7 security
8 entrance
9 reception
10 meeting room
11 lift lobby
12 bathroom
13 break-out space
14 office
15 quiet room

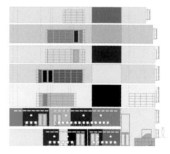

section

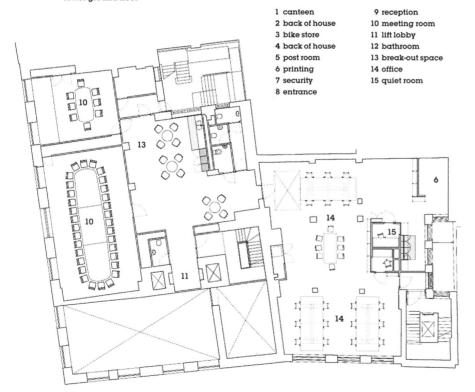

upper ground floor

The Potterrow development is not just part of a university campus, it is also the realization of a master plan in this area of the Scottish capital. Formerly a car park, the site separates a busy road to the east from a pedestrian route to the west that connects Edinburgh city centre and Bristo Square to the historic George Square, itself subjected to some notorious demolitions in the 1960s. And Potterrow has earned its green stripes courtesy of a BREEAM Excellent rating too.

The first phase of the project was made up of two parts – the Informatics Forum and the Dugald Stewart Building. The former is home to around 500 researchers, who comprise the School of Informatics. This complex subject encompasses artificial intelligence, psychology, maths, biology and social sciences. One objective of the development was to provide a workplace that would attract the best academics in the discipline, and promote their ability to work, both independently and, crucially, in collaboration.

A striking feature of the informatics building is that the height varies in different parts. The atrium, accessed through a large timber door, effortlessly gives the entrance the 'wow' factor, and instantly shows the most important characteristic of the office at work – its break-out spaces. Here, academics can take the time to meet informally. Even the show-stopping 'wormholes' – staircases for ease of access between floors – are intended to encourage chance encounters through the vertical integration of different departments. Photocopier/printer areas are deliberately not separated off into their own rooms, and kitchens are extended into social spaces for the same reason. The corridors between the cellular research labs and offices are spaciously appointed to allow for casual conversation as others pass by.

A steel-framed link incorporates stairs, lifts and a coffee lounge at every level. The lower flat roofs of the building are used as gardens and have picturesque views of Edinburgh Castle. Seemingly, the weather provides no obstacle to barbecues for yet more team bonding. Due care was taken to ensure the building blended well with its surroundings. Along Potterrow, one of the development's perimeter streets, the building is a well-mannered four storeys, and pre-cast panels of natural stone respond well to neighbouring buildings.

POTTERROW DEVELOPMENT, UNIVERSITY OF EDINBURGH

Architect: **Bennetts Associates**
Client: **University of Edinburgh**
Location: **Edinburgh, UK**
Completed: **June 2008**
Size: **16,500 sq m (177,610 sq ft)**
Budget: **£41.2 million**

The project's environmental impact was important to both client and architects. Displacement air is supplied at ground-floor level and the exposed concrete structure provides thermal mass, while rainwater harvesting, mixed ventilation, a façade that allows for good daylight, and a combined heat and power system all help to add to Potterrow's green kudos.

This is the first phase of a major redevelopment. Phase 2 is another departmental building facing onto an internal courtyard, covered in white cast stone and planted with birch trees. Phase 3 will complete the courtyard and form the Potterrow 'street', a road that reinterprets the historic street pattern demolished in the 1960s.

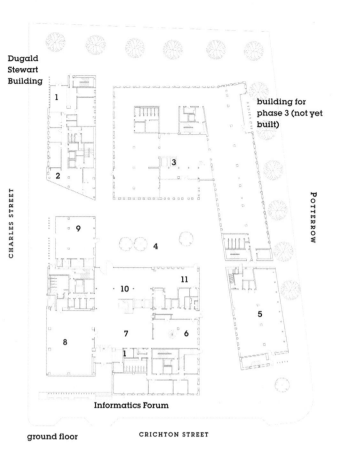

Dugald
Stewart
Building

building for
phase 3 (not yet
built)

CHARLES STREET

POTTERROW

1   reception
2   break-out area
3   atrium
4   courtyard
5   exhibition space
6   robotics lab
7   forum/break-out area
8   meeting room
9   visitor centre
10   café
11   conference room
12   coffee point
13   informal meeting area
14   'wormhole' staircases
15   area for visiting academics
16   group study area
17   print area
18   roof terrace
19   seminar rooms
20   outdoor meeting area

Page 240: Visitors and staff alike access the building by the same entrance and are welcomed by this huge atrium space, which provides a dramatic first impression.

Left: The Dugald Stewart Building and the Informatics Forum are the first stage in the three-phase development of Potterrow. **Below**: The whole development contains a mix of private offices, formal meeting rooms and more informal break-out spaces.

Opposite: An outside terrace offers spectacular views of the Edinburgh landscape (*top left*). The building's glass frontage lets the maximum amount of daylight into the building and so keeps the use of artificial lighting to a minimum (*top right*). Staircases, likened to 'wormholes', have been designed to encourage chance encounters between academics from different departments (*bottom left*). Potterrow is built on what was once a car park in the Scottish capital (*bottom right*).

Informatics Forum

ground floor

CRICHTON STREET

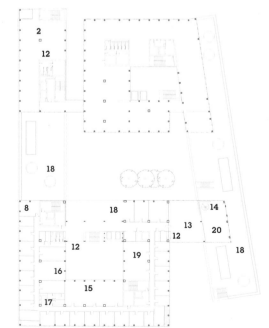

fourth floor

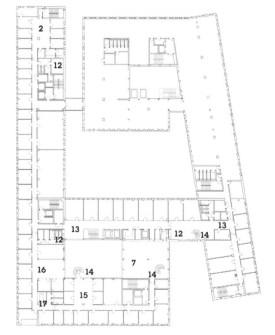

second floor

When its premises in Johannesburg's city centre could no longer cope with its space requirements FNB HomeLoans decided to move to an area known as Jerusalem in the city's suburbs. Once this decision became public, it prompted the interest of the asset management company WesBank, which followed suit in deciding to build new facilities in the Jerusalem area; part of the enterprise included a shared venue for entertaining. The site had been used as an illegal dump and housed many squatters. The decision to create an office campus there necessarily involved support from the local community, and extensive consultation was carried out to ensure that the development was acceptable to the residents.

The urban design and planning had to pay attention to the natural world and integrate it into the project. Part of the solution to these demands is the 'Path in the Veld', a planted passage of greenery, winding its way across the site. As water is considered the most precious element in Africa, and also has spiritual significance, the three interlinked buildings were conceived as a 'body of water', a metaphor for the homogeneity of the workforce, whose members must interact in order to survive.

The floor plans of WesBank and FNB HomeLoan's individual buildings are characterized by very large floor plates (about 15,000 sq m and 11,000 sq m per floor respectively), allowing for a high degree of integration between the different departments in each company. The largest component of WesBank's business is the inbound and outbound call centre, which operates 24 hours a day, 365 days a year, on a local and national level. The basement houses the workaday elements of the scheme, including car-parking space for 1,600, storage facilities, a gym, and computer and electrical rooms, as well as back-of-house facilities for the kitchens.

The part of the project shared by FNB HomeLoans and WesBank comprises some 3,000 sq m, dedicated to recreation and dining. This multifunctional venue can be used for three different functions simultaneously, and includes a 600-seat auditorium and a banqueting facility for up to 400. The ceiling of the banqueting hall is patterned in the form of floating lily pads, with light

FAIRLANDS OFFICE

Architect: **Continuum Architects**
Client: **FNB HomeLoans and WesBank**
Location: **Johannesburg, South Africa**
Completed: **March 2008**
Site area: **160,000 sq m (1,722,230 sq ft)**
Budget: **undisclosed**

fittings representing bubbles; the design is intended to give the feeling of submersion.

The main method of controlling energy consumption was to insulate the buildings in myriad ways. Passive control measures include double-glazed windows, insulated walls and roofs, and exoskeleton sunscreens.

Providing some cultural context was part of the design brief. Since the advent of democracy in South Africa in 1994, financial institutions have been seen as lifestyle partners, embracing the notion of 'identity in diversity'. An outreach programme involved local children in making sketches and potato prints based on the word 'knowledge'. Their work, using the earthy tones of the African landscape, was then laminated and used as sunscreen panels on the eight façades. Fire-escape stairs reference local baobab trees and together with the vertical sunscreens give the impression of reeds next to water.

Page 244: The entrance features an atmospheric graphic of the South African landscape to characterize the building's strong connection with its location.

Above: The site contains three interlinked buildings: FNB HomeLoans, WesBank and a shared facility.

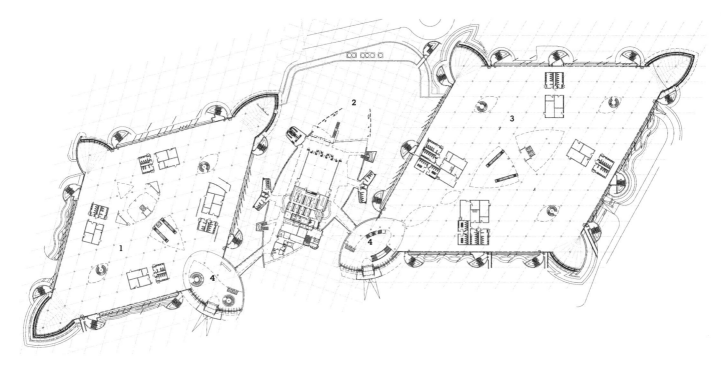

ground floor

1   FNB HomeLoans building
2   shared facilities
3   WesBank building
4   main atriums
5   planted boulevard

Opposite: The building is a large-scale
campus environment and the ground-
floor space is divided using semi-private,
birdcage-like structures and lighting
(*bottom right*). The designers used a
palette of earthy colours to connect the
building to the natural world (*bottom left*).
It was also important to include plants
within the workspace to provide another
reference point to the greenery outside
(*top right*). Even the ceiling is designed
to resemble floating lily pads (*top left*).

Above: Each of the office buildings
adjoins a connecting area that houses
shared facilities. **Right**: The vast site
features a planted boulevard that winds
its way through a seemingly natural and
indigenous landscape.

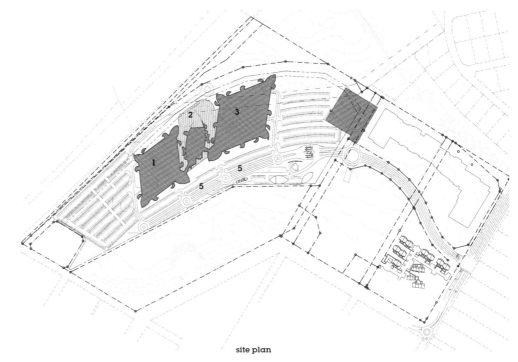

site plan

Pages 250–51: Visitors and staff alike are treated to a dramatic staircase, which leads down to the break-out space.

Above left: The pendant lights work to soften the design of this large corporate environment. **Above right**: The illuminated, circular reception desk provides a theatrical design statement in the entrance to the building. **Left**: FNB HomeLoans and WesBank share facilities, this includes dining areas in one of the three interlinked buildings.

Opposite: The entrance to the WesBank building has a light, airy feel.

Boston-based DesignLAB worked on the new headquarters for the international non-profit organization IFAW, the world's leading animal welfare organization. The client wanted a workplace that would be ecologically sustainable, and respectful of its context and location on Cape Cod, Massachusetts. The resulting building, on a brownfield site from which the client had removed quantities of detritus, used simple, unadorned farm buildings that are typical of the area – two-storey barn-like structures, or sheds, with white clapboard cladding. The office project even includes an undulating meadow with native trees and bushes to recreate the Cape Cod area's natural beauty.

The sheds are designed as sunlight-filled, open-plan places, which can be easily reconfigured, with generous views outside. They are arranged around a courtyard, which serves as a centrepiece for the headquarters. Open staircases punctuate the walkway along the meadow, encouraging dialogue and collaboration among employees. All the service spaces – work rooms, restrooms, copier rooms – are integrated into a service bar opposite the courtyard. This arrangement avoids unnecessary disruption of the open-plan working environment. Work rooms and smaller 'conversation' rooms are also there, allowing opportunities for staff to brainstorm, hold confidential discussions or make private phone calls.

A series of brightly coloured conference rooms provide landmarks within the space, each branded with images from one of IFAW's campaigns or key environmental strategies. At the main entrance, a resource lounge gives visitors a handy introduction to IFAW's work, including an interactive video display. The workplace also incorporates an exhibit trail, which weaves through the building.

Materials are clean and crisp with white wood cladding and zinc-coated metal roofing, which is intended to weather to a soft grey. The meadow at the centre of the building is surrounded by full-height transparent and frit glass, layered in jarrah shutters, and open wooden decks. Other materials used include ceramic wall and floor tiles and rubber flooring. Many of the building materials are sustainable, including some of the structural steel, window framing and foundation insulation: 91% of the wood used in construction was harvested from managed forests.

IFAW HEADQUARTERS

Architect: **DesignLAB**
Client: **International Fund for Animal Welfare (IFAW)**
Location: **Yarmouth Port, MA, USA**
Completed: **January 2008**
Size: **5,020 sq m (54,000 sq ft)**
Budget: **US $12.5 million**

IFAW headquarters is designed to use 45% less energy for heating and air conditioning and nearly a quarter less energy for lighting than similar buildings. This is achieved through an air-conditioning system cooled by evaporation and a high-efficiency gas-fuelled condensing boiler, as well as state-of-the-art fluorescent lighting.

Among the most notable other green features are the bioswales and rain gardens, designed to channel, collect and cleanse rainwater runoff from the car park. This feature, along with those previously mentioned, led to the building being selected by the American Institute of Architects (AIA) and its Committee on the Environment as one of the top ten examples of sustainable architecture and green design in 2009.

1 exterior boardwalk
2 interior boardwalk
3 conference room
4 café
5 reception lounge
6 open offices
7 support spaces
8 balcony
9 courtyard

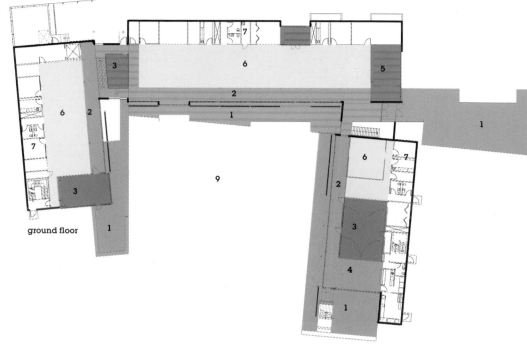

ground floor

Page 254: The building is made up of two-storey barn-like structures that really let in the sunlight.

Page 256–57: The office is located on a brownfield site in a picturesque part of Cape Cod.

Above: On the ground floor, a timber interior walkway runs parallel to the exterior boardwalk. These walkways surround three sides of the undulating meadow shown on pages 256–57.
Right: Balconies at each end of the building allow staff to enjoy the landscape's natural beauty.

Opposite: Many of the building materials used were sustainable, including the structural steel, the window frames and the insulation for the walls (*top left*). The American animal charity's office features windows with jarrah wood shutters (*bottom right*). Graphics that take nature as their theme reinforce the designer's aim of creating an eco-friendly aesthetic throughout the interior (*bottom left*); depictions of animals have been used in this meeting room (*top right*).

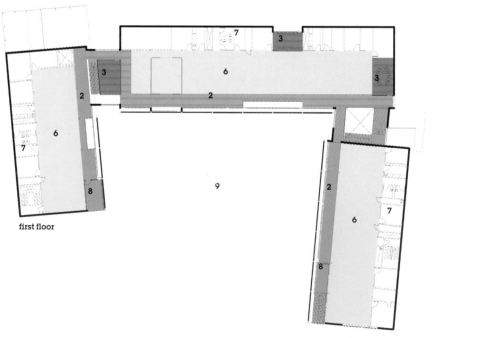

first floor

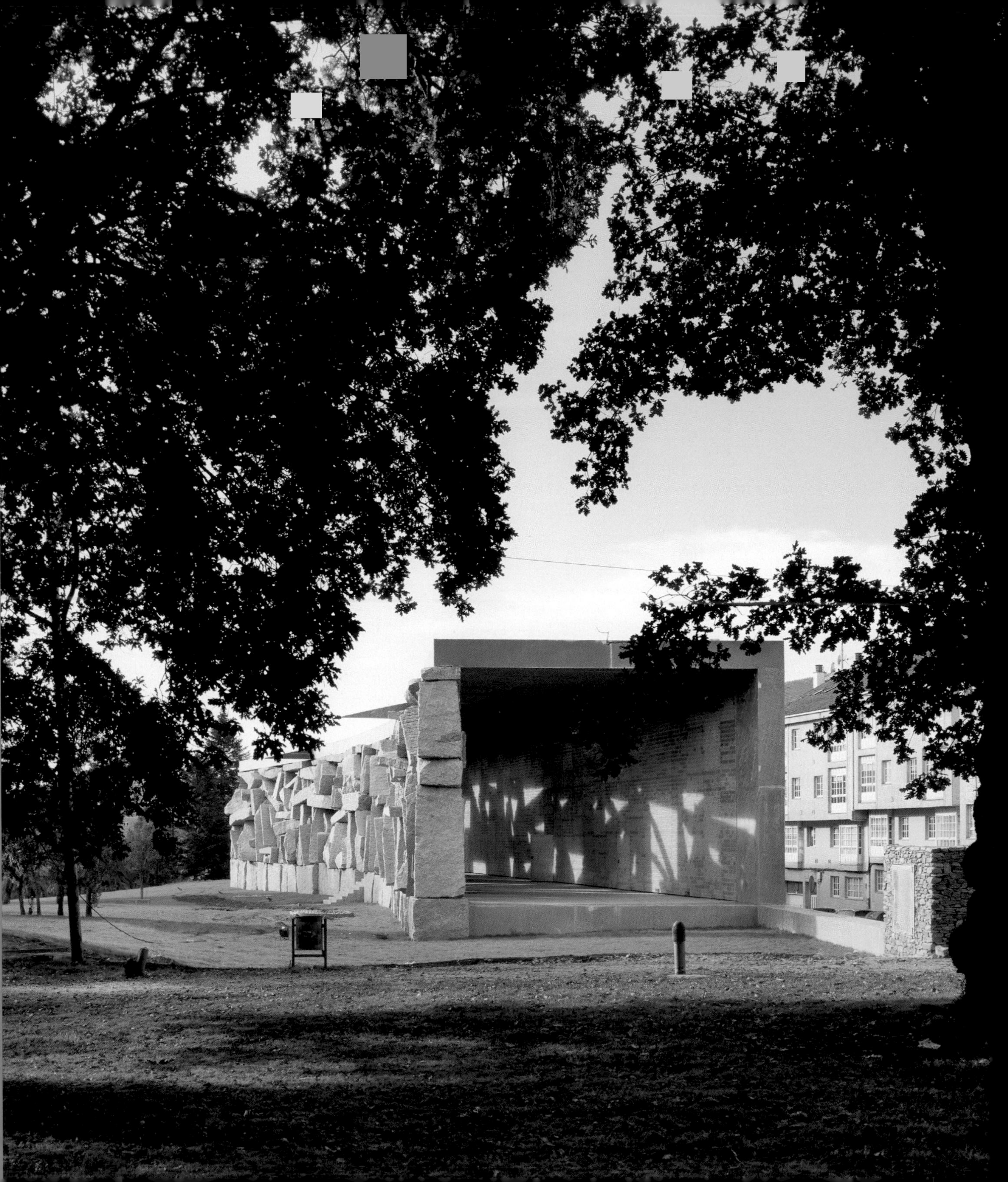

The offices of the SGAE, Spain's general society of authors and publishers, are a striking construction of stone slabs, located on the western limits of the city of Santiago de Compostela. The plot was developed by the Japanese architect Arata Isozaki, who came up with the initial blueprint for a series of buildings for academic use. SGAE's office is located in the west of the plot and was designed by Ensamble Studio. The architecture is intended to reference the spirit of the city – the history of Santiago, the Galician landscape and ancient culture – as well as upholding a sense of what twenty-first-century design means.

The SGAE not only arranges social activities for authors and publishers, but also organizes a range of other cultural events. The building has a private garden on one side and a green space on the other, while the city's medieval buildings are visible on the skyline. The workspace is divided into four functional areas, including one for management and another that is accessible to the public from the garden and the street. A stone wall made of Gris Mondariz looks out over the garden. This Spanish grey granite, with its irregular shapes and sizes, has a sculptural quality reminiscent of prehistoric constructions. The stones are assembled in such a way as to manipulate the light from the south to utilize natural daylight as much as possible.

Between the stone wall and a translucent glass wall that faces the street is an interior wall, clad in used CDs, which draws an arc between the two, cutting through the colossal scale of the workspace. The reflective quality of the CDs makes the partition shimmer like a stained-glass window, and the play of colours and light offers a contrast with the natural robustness and opacity of the stone. The glass wall controls the view onto and in from the street, filtering the light and veiling the activities going on inside.

These three materials contrast and interact, echoing the irregular, fluid spaces that they define. Typical of the subtle references the building makes is the arcaded walkway between the CD wall and the stone wall, which conjures up the streets of the city. This narrows towards the middle of the building, where the main entrance is situated. At each end of the walkway the exterior landscape is visible, framed by openings in the outer walls, so that a double aspect may be seen from any point along its length.

SGAE OFFICES

Architect: **Ensamble Studio**
Client: **SGAE**
Location: **Santiago de Compostela, Spain**
Completed: **January 2007**
Size: **4,000 sq m (43,060 sq ft)**
Budget: **€8 million**

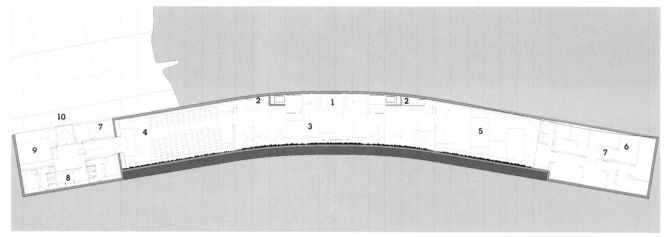

basement floor (4 m below ground level)

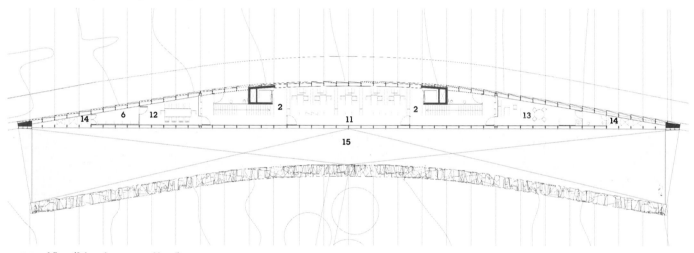

ground floor (0.4 m above ground level)

1 recording booth
2 vertical communication core
3 multipurpose space
4 auditorium
5 multipurpose set
6 storage
7 facilities
8 dressing room
9 garage
10 access
11 administration
12 boardroom
13 office
14 building services
15 porticoed street

Page 260: The offices are composed of a series of slabs of Gris Mondariz, a Spanish grey granite.

Top: The gently curving building includes two floors underground. This level, 4 metres below ground, features an auditorium. **Above**: The porticoed 'street' space takes up a large proportion of the building. It is bordered by a stone wall that faces onto the garden.

Opposite: The stone wall juxtaposed with the translucent glass creates an interesting contrast between traditional and modern materials (*top left*). The building's stone slabs have been arranged and manipulated to maximize the available daylight (*bottom left*). Brighter hues, used in the interior, give a contemporary, warm feeling to the office (*bottom right*). Bold tiling has been used in one of the workspace's four functional areas (*top right*).

Vodafone Headquarters/Barbosa & Guimarães

This show-stopping office build already has iconic written all over it. Vodafone's new Portuguese headquarters has a solid, monumental presence, yet manages to convey a sense of movement. This effect was at the core of Barbosa & Guimarães' design concept, which won a competition to build the high-profile project. The Portuguese architects began with Vodafone's slogan, 'Vodafone life, life in motion', as the principle behind their design, and developed a concrete structure that embodies that motion.

The headquarters occupies eight floors (three of these underground), and can house 250 employees. The building instantly makes a lasting impression with its sculptural surface: the façade is composed of granite and concrete slabs, designed as irregular shapes, inset with asymmetrical windows. Inside the building there are no right angles, which creates a dynamic that breaks with the common linearity of standard offices. Yet the construction methods were kept simple, and the complexity of the technical design was achieved by using a strong peripheral structure. The build itself consists of a reinforced concrete egg-like shell, which distributes the weight and allows internal support mechanisms to be reduced – three pillars and two stairwells are the only internal support structures, creating space for the open-plan office floors.

The landmark character of the headquarters holds obvious appeal for the client, but the most beneficial result of the stunning design is the effect it has on Vodafone staff members. Natural daylight zigzags throughout the building like lightning bolts, entering through the irregular windows and skylights, and creates a sense of momentum within the interior. The space encourages constant movement, which today's workplace strategists believe is the healthiest way of working, as it alleviates the strains of sitting at a desk, for both body and mind, and this flow and motion creates happier, healthier and more efficient staff.

Certainly, a structure of this ingenuity will meet with mixed opinions, but the design is not meant to be shocking, and Barbosa & Guimarães paid a great deal of attention to the surrounding environment when conceiving their project. The building is in line with other architectural gems in Porto, including Rem Koolhaas's white concrete Casa da Musica concert hall. The architects kept the Vodafone headquarters in check with neighbouring buildings by restricting the height to 19 metres, so that it would not dwarf the structures in the immediate vicinity. Consequently, three underground floors house the car park and technical areas. Uneven terraces and an unusual garden above ground add to the sense that this building might be on a different planet, but who wouldn't want to work in an office that is out of this world?

VODAFONE HEADQUARTERS

Architect: **Barbosa & Guimarães**
Client: **Vodafone**
Location: **Porto, Portugal**
Completed: **November 2009**
Size: **7,470 sq m (80,430 sq ft)**
Budget: **€11.5 million**

Page 264: The craggy sculptural façade of the Vodafone office conjures up images of glaciers and galactic mountain ranges.

Below and right: Diamond-shaped windows zigzag across the front of the concrete monolith: the objective was to create a building that echoes the dynamic character of Vodafone's business.

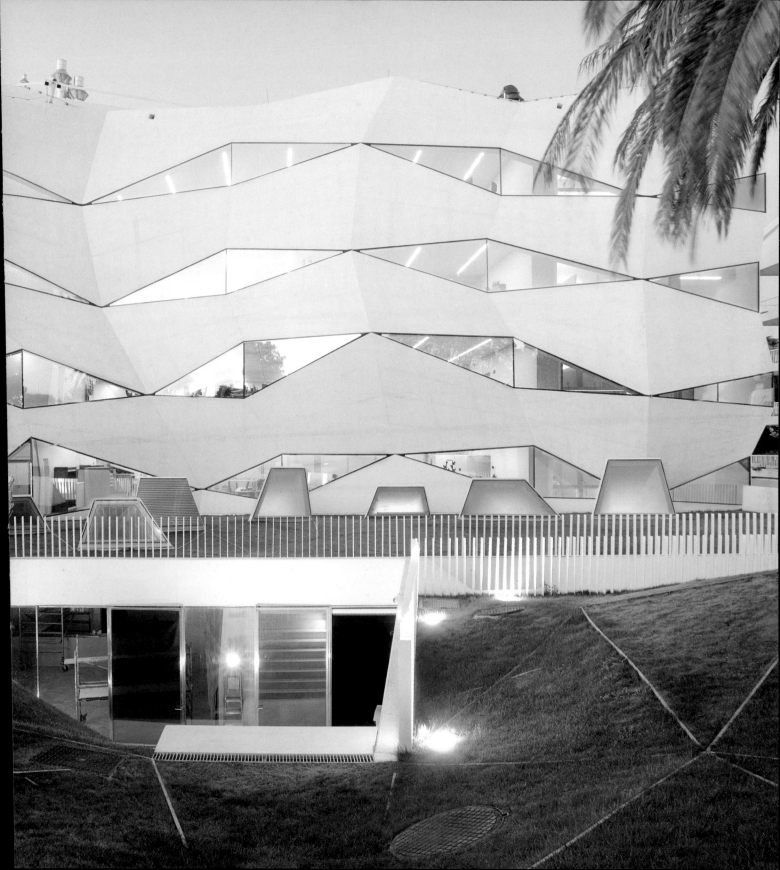

cross-section

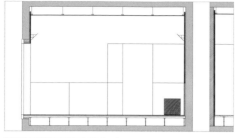

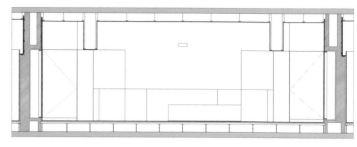

section

floor plan

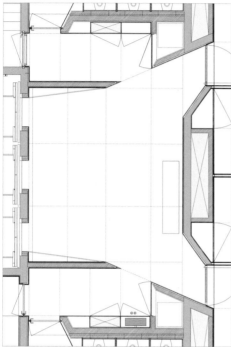

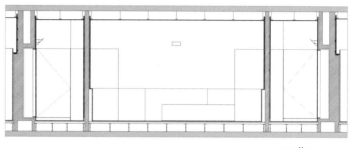

section

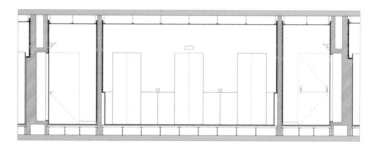

section

This page: Despite the space-age exterior, the interior floor plan is relatively conventional. The office is laid out over eight floors, three of them below ground for parking. Structurally, the building has a reinforced-concrete shell; internal supports consist of three central pillars and two stairwells. The height of the new offices was matched to the architectural context (*below*) so as not to dwarf surrounding buildings.

Opposite: The interior design is minimalist and the decor cool: the only hint of the radical exterior is the asymmetrical double triangles that form the window slots.

section

Left: Spacious workstations are positioned along continuous desking, divided by low vertical screens. The offices are flooded with natural light from the large windows. **Below**: The stairwell, which sensationally avoids right angles as it rises through the space, emulates the wacky geometry of the outside of the building. On the ceiling, all light fittings have been positioned inside black teardrop shapes painted onto the surface, obscuring the straight lines of the light fixtures and emphasizing the absence of right angles in the space.

Newham Council, which administers the large borough of Newham in East London, formerly had staff working in twenty-four separate buildings. It wanted a new headquarters to consolidate all its activities on one site, accommodating 2,500 people. The purpose-built office space extends over eight floors in the Royal Albert Docks, near London City airport.

At the start of the project, one objective was to switch to hotdesking. Interior designers ID:SR completed an activity analysis to put a figure on exactly how much time staff spent away from their desks. They discovered that a ratio of 10:7 (that is, ten staff to seven desks) would accommodate the council's needs, which frees up 25% of the floor plate. Careful consultation with employees and effective negotiation have resulted in cost savings. Originally, staff had wanted curving desk clusters, but this arrangement would only accommodate 198 people per floor, compared with as many as 240 using straight lines of desks.

Essentially, the workspace combines compact desk areas with high-quality varied meeting areas. The new reception area is sleek and corporate, its first impression competing with that given by any blue-chip firm; shocking pink, white and timber dominate. The adjacent meeting rooms provide an environment suitable for professional dialogue with local businesses and other boroughs.

This interior hardly feels cramped though: there are plenty of places to go aside from the workstations. The purple 'town square' areas are intended for more formal gatherings and town hall meetings. Dominating the decor, meanwhile, is a ribbon made of beech, an independent structure that follows the perimeter of the floors, and provides a screen for the workstation clusters. Within this structure there are various meeting and working opportunities, from the 'bus stops', intended as highly informal gathering places, through to the study spaces for quieter work.

Contrasting with the timber, jewel-like pinks and oranges have been deployed to add a playful element to the working environment. Within the colours there are patterns referencing the borough's ethnic diversity, which support the idea of this office being a real 'community' that serves a community.

The concept of community is perhaps best exemplified by the 'park' areas, where staff can have lunch and meet

NEWHAM COUNCIL HEADQUARTERS

Architect: **ID:SR**
Client: **Newham Council**
Location: **London, UK**
Completed: **June 2009**
Size: **23,000 sq m (247,570 sq ft)**
Budget: **undisclosed**

informally. They are furnished with cosy clusters of tables and chairs and softer seating in various shades of green. This multifunctionality was crucial in fulfilling the part of the brief that called for collaborative working and chance encounters.

In developing its new facility, Newham Council had a number of different objectives, besides the added efficiency of consolidating its staff on one site. It has rationalized its assets, reducing its property costs by 30%, and has proved its green credentials by cutting its carbon output by the same amount.

Page 272: Large-scale graphics of people help to promote the idea that the council works for the diverse community.

Below: A large amount of the ground floor is taken up by café and restaurant space – a place for the community of workers to socialize and work in a more relaxed atmosphere. **Bottom**: Desks are arranged in straight lines to maximize the amount of space available for different kinds of working areas – informal meeting rooms, break-out and touchdown zones – encouraging alternative ways of working.

Opposite: Staff can have lunch or meet informally in 'park' areas (*top left*). The café and restaurant areas, on the ground floor of the building, provide a number of dining options with contemporary furnishings (*top and bottom right*). Colour helps to guide people around the building, as well as developing an engaging workplace design aesthetic (*bottom left*).

1 facilities management/business support area
2 business centre: boardroom, training rooms, meeting rooms, interview rooms, reception/waiting area
3 restaurant and café
4 coffee bar
5 'ribbon': touchdown desks, coat cupboards, meeting rooms, filing, tea points
6 desks
7 'park' area
8 meeting area
9 arrival zone
10 break-out/touchdown area
11 high-density filing

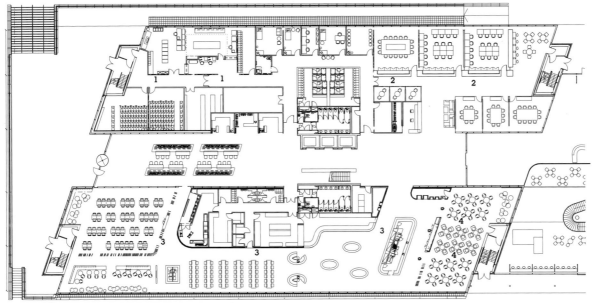

ground floor

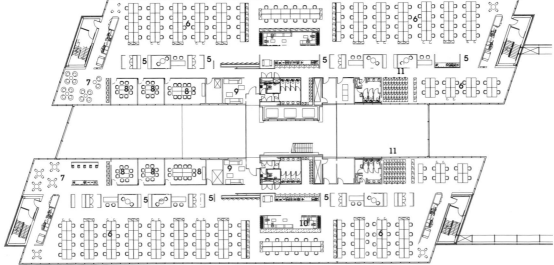

first floor

The refurbished Steckelhörn 11 office complex is a special project situated in the historic centre of Hamburg. It is the second workplace designed by Jürgen Mayer H. in Hamburg, following the celebrated ADA1 office building completed in 2007. It is no coincidence that both offices have been built in collaboration with Cogiton, a property firm run by the ambitious developer Andreas Barke, who only builds one-off designs, and aims to establish a clear connection between his various developments. Barke sees his buildings as products not projects, and refers to them as artworks rather than offices.

Wedged in between two listed buildings, the oddly shaped nine-storey building block posed a challenge due to its unusual dimensions: one side stretches only 1.3 metres, while the front façade covers 26.4 metres. As a result of these limitations, the triangular layout had previously housed a dark and dingy space. In response to the demands of the site, Jürgen Mayer H. focused on bringing light into the building, using numerous glass casements, each of which also frames one of Hamburg's many iconic sights. The narrow end that used to back onto a canal outlines the harbour and the new Herzog & de Meuron Elbphilharmonie concert hall, while the front section allows views of the restored St Katharinen church on one side and the town hall on the other.

The building has two sides to the front façade because it follows the historic curve of Steckelhörn street. The architects focused on seamlessly slotting the refurbished block into the neighbouring buildings; through the creation of a cascading wave-optic façade, the ceramic-clad front smoothes out the bend. The chocolate-coloured ceramic façade flows down over the building like a waterfall, evoking parallels to its location at the old harbour, along the banks of the river Elbe. In the sun, this breathtaking vertical cascade sparkles like gold.

A holistic vision ties the interior and exterior together in a seamless finish. The inside of the office, like the outside, is an uninterrupted surface with no edges or corners – from the cast-plastic flush features to the Corian columns emerging subtly from the floor. A single, consistent design language flows throughout the space, managing to avoid repetition by relying on reinterpretations of the shapes of

S11 OFFICE COMPLEX

Architect: **Jürgen Mayer H.**
Client: **Cogiton Projekt Altstadt**
Location: **Hamburg, Germany**
Completed: **November 2009**
Size: **3,000 sq m (32,290 sq ft)**
Budget: **undisclosed**

recurring fixtures, such as light sockets. The chocolate of the façade is echoed in the interior colour palette in various shades of brown. The only deliberate break from this unobtrusive colour scheme is found in the building's two lifts, designed in deliberately contrasting bright pink.

Even with all of the successful details, the most striking feature of the building remains the engagement with its unusually angled layout; inside, the placement of meeting rooms, and even individual desks, provides the workforce with surprising views. The architects have deliberately created suspense, designing an office space devoid of boring vistas. Interestingly, the developers have profited from the triangular shape of the building as the floor plan allows a higher occupancy per square metre than the usual German office, with twenty-two to thirty-two people on each floor over 420 sq metres – all without the space ever seeming congested.

Page 276: The ceramic panels that decorate the surface of the S11 building in Hamburg flow down the façade like a series of narrow waterfalls.

Above left and opposite: The back of the building measures a mere 1.3 m while the front stretches across 26.4 m. At the rear, S11 is no more than a slot wedged into a small gap between two classic examples of Hanseatic architecture. **Above right**: The ceramic cladding that coats the building gleams in the sun. **Left**: The undulating contours of the building, highlighted by the cascading decorative features, evokes associations with the sea and references the nearby harbour where the ships ride at anchor. **Right**: The model shows how the S11 development (outlined in red) is wedged between two listed buildings, forming a triangular shape.

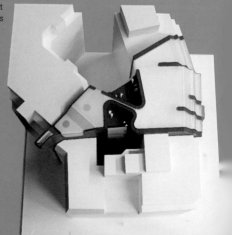

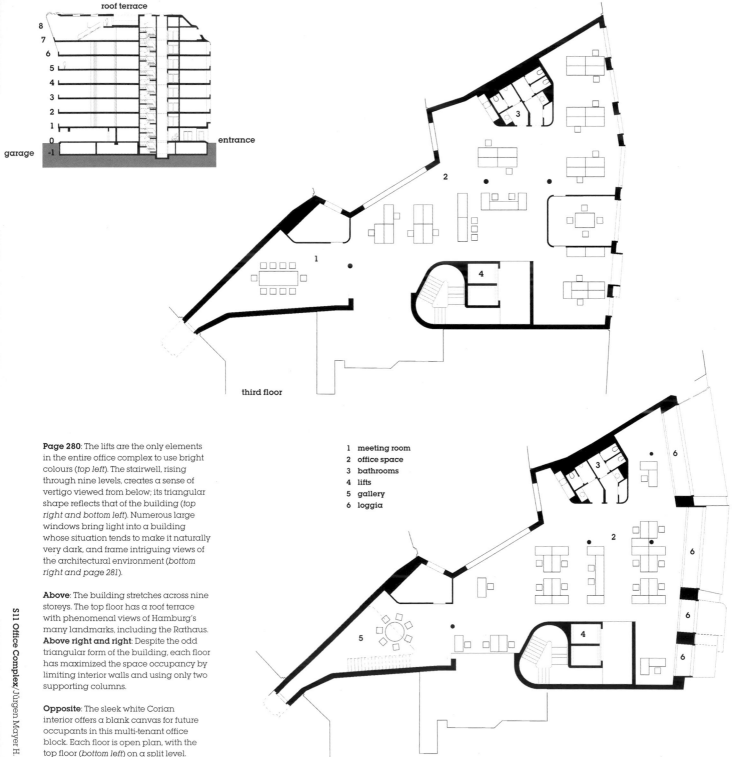

roof terrace

8
7
6
5
4
3
2
1
0
-1

garage

entrance

third floor

Page 280: The lifts are the only elements in the entire office complex to use bright colours (*top left*). The stairwell, rising through nine levels, creates a sense of vertigo viewed from below; its triangular shape reflects that of the building (*top right and bottom left*). Numerous large windows bring light into a building whose situation tends to make it naturally very dark, and frame intriguing views of the architectural environment (*bottom right and page 281*).

Above: The building stretches across nine storeys. The top floor has a roof terrace with phenomenal views of Hamburg's many landmarks, including the Rathaus.
Above right and right: Despite the odd triangular form of the building, each floor has maximized the space occupancy by limiting interior walls and using only two supporting columns.

Opposite: The sleek white Corian interior offers a blank canvas for future occupants in this multi-tenant office block. Each floor is open plan, with the top floor (*bottom left*) on a split level.

1 meeting room
2 office space
3 bathrooms
4 lifts
5 gallery
6 loggia

seventh floor

The design for the MTC Inversions office complex is all about bridging the gap between the urban outskirts of Rubí and its surrounding riverside landscape. After all, today's sustainable architecture goes beyond using green building materials – it is increasingly about coherence between a build and its immediate environment. Barcelona-based architects Bailo and Rull, from ADD + ARQUITECTURA, designed this contemporary office to reference the natural surroundings, creating a design that offers as much visually for those viewing it from the exterior as for the staff working inside. Known in Spain for developing basic buildings with striking façades, for example Garden House 0.96, Manuel Bailo Esteve and Rosa Rull Bertran set out to give this manufacturing base a touch of magic.

Due to the modest budget, the architects decided to use a prefabricated system with pre-cast concrete at the office's core. This freed up enough of the budget to develop a special façade design for the outer shell, which addressed the project's main goal of establishing a natural relationship between the office exterior and its direct environment. The façade is an ornate skin characterized by a random mix of flat and angled slabs that resonate with the shade of stone and granite found in the area. These slabs were prefabricated at the same plant as the pre-cast concrete, which kept their cost down considerably, and, despite their low price, they have a big impact on the office's visual make-up. In addition to linking the building to the landscape, the façade's structural system also mirrors the style of the neighbouring warehouses and the general aesthetic of the adjoining industrial zone.

ADD describe the design concept as an 'artificial garden'. From inside the MTC office, the angled window slots offer enticing views of the surrounding landscape. The positioning of the window shields varies throughout the day: concrete slabs function as shutters and rotate with the movement of the sun, bringing the façade alive. From inside, each window-bay frames a different view of the surrounding landscape, and as the slabs gradually shift position during the day, the vista changes. As a result, patterns are formed on the interior surfaces – another link to the world outside. Natural light floods each floor and eco-friendly light tubes, charged by the solar panels on the roof, transmit daylight

MTC INVERSIONS OFFICE

Architect: **bailo + rull / ADD + ARQUITECTURA**
Client: **MTC Inversions**
Location: **Rubí, Spain**
Completed: **April 2008**
Size: **3,580 sq m (38,500 sq ft)**
Budget: **€1.9 million**

through large glass screens that act as space dividers. These screens are covered in vinyl printed with images of the local plant life in keeping with the garden theme. Yet the interior is simultaneously defined by a single industrial process: the pre-cast concrete, which lends itself to the feel of a manufacturing plant. MTC Inversions manufacture technological equipment and it is that reality, interwoven with images of wildlife on the screens, and the natural landscape, that creates a healthy environment for workers.

The interior provides a high level of flexibility: the concrete shell easily facilitates various floor-plan solutions as there are no columns or walls to divide the space. Instead, freestanding glass screens can be rearranged to create work clusters. All this gives the furniture system the potential to change configuration and upgrades it to an architectural level, where it defines the space. Centrally located electrics and services add to this flexibility and help make the management of space a straightforward process.

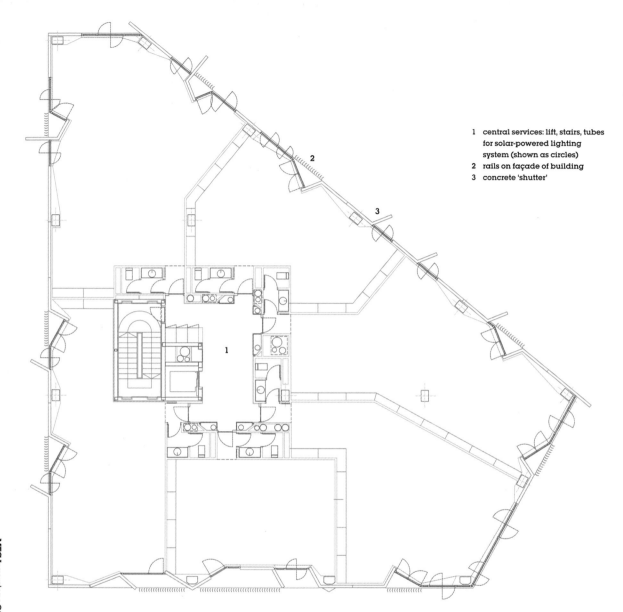

1 central services: lift, stairs, tubes
  for solar-powered lighting
  system (shown as circles)
2 rails on façade of building
3 concrete 'shutter'

Page 284: Located on the edge of an industrial area, MTC's office aims to bridge the gap between concrete building and the surrounding natural greenery.

Above: The facilities – including the electrics, the lifts and the solar lighting system that illuminates the vinyl panels (*opposite, bottom left*) – are grouped in the centre of the space, leaving the work floor open and allowing views through the many shuttered windows to dominate the rooms.

Opposite: Plant imagery is digitally printed onto glass screens that function as space dividers. The prefabricated concrete slabs on the exterior skin are positioned at different angles to work as shutters throughout the day. The view of the natural habitat is part of the interior's appeal.

3FOLD designed the new home for the Student Loans Company, a public sector organization that processes student loan applications for higher education in the UK. The 'contact and processing centre' is located in a former thread-making factory at Lingfield Point business park in Darlington, in northeast England.

The designers made the social spine of the workplace an integral part of the space. There are tea and coffee areas and a café fitted with laptop points to enable staff and visitors to plug in and work. What had been the bathroom block was transformed into a recreational space with benches, table football and a plasma screen to enable staff to relax during break periods.

In order to promote a sense of community within the large open-plan office space, the workstations have been grouped into smaller teams of about twelve people, and are easily identified by lettering in splashes of different citrus colours. Because the nature of the work means that there are often spikes of activity, bench-type work settings have added flexibility in the use of the space and can accommodate a 30% increase in staff without moving or adding any additional seating. Each of the 670 staff members has also been designated a personal locker, allowing for additional flexibility in changing over workstations.

For more private meetings, there are twelve pod spaces furnished with sofas and screens. The boardroom, meanwhile, is fitted with acoustic panels and the glass partitioning can be switched from clear to opaque when required.

While there's no getting away from the fact that this office was once a factory – the building's layout and large windows that allow in plenty of natural light serve as reminders – the present is very much reconciled with the past. Contemporary culture is referenced in the skateboard ramp-like meeting spaces with long benches. The modern aesthetic and plentiful meeting areas already go a long way to making this call space seem a lot less like a typical call-centre environment. To further achieve this distinction, 3FOLD used textures and colours very different from those expected in a corporate office, which both delight and surprise the users. These include TeCrete concrete access tiles, magnetic rubber floor tiles, and grass-coloured carpet tiles, all complemented by colourful furniture.

STUDENT LOANS COMPANY OFFICE

Architect: **3FOLD**
Client: **The Student Loans Company**
Location: **Darlington, UK**
Completed: **June 2008**
Size: **5,300 sq m (57,070 sq ft)**
Budget: **£8.5 million**

Sustainability is a big part of the story too. Shower facilities and bike racks encourage people to cycle to work, while a low-energy light management system uses sensors to balance out the amount of natural daylight available, and solar panels on the roof provide heating for water. These features, combined with recyclable materials such as rubber on the freestanding partition screens and natural materials like cork, make this office playful and green at the same time. The Student Loans Company office was awarded a BCO (British Council for Offices) Regional Award for Refurbished/Recycled workspace in 2009 in recognition of 3FOLD's creative overhaul of the space.

1 terrace
2 store
3 post room
4 communications
5 coffee point
6 reception
7 interview room
8 meeting room
9 boardroom
10 training room
11 learning space

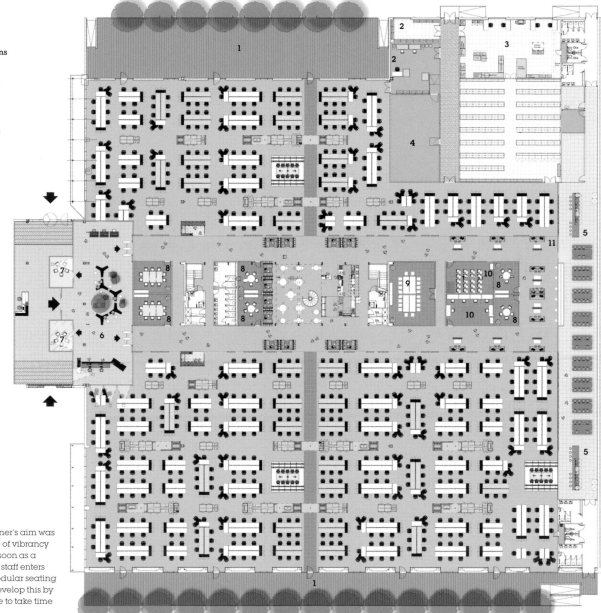

floor plate

Page 288: The designer's aim was to engender a sense of vibrancy and community as soon as a visitor or member of staff enters the building; the modular seating shown here helps develop this by encouraging people to take time out and talk.

Above: Meeting, eating and breakout space running down the centre of the floor plate form the 'social spine' of the office.

Opposite: Workstations have been organized into small groups. The design is generously proportioned, which means more staff can be added to the desks during busy periods.

Right: A hub of break-out space, part of a social spine running through the centre of the office. This spine's floor is a rich chocolate brown, marking it off from the working area opposite.

Below: Staff were moved from a number of different locations to this purpose-designed workplace, which contains playful features like the texture on the walls.

This page and opposite: Staff can relax in comfort in booth-style seating during their breaks (*opposite, top left*). Each team has its own storage provision (*opposite, top right*) and each member of staff has their own locker; this offers workers possibilities to work in different places. Individual teams can be identified through bold lettering and graphics (*below left*). Café areas feature citrus shades to help pep up staff energy levels (*left*). The stylish modern furnishings differentiate this office from other local call-centre employers (*below right*). The grey-upholstered, high-backed seating areas can be used as places to hold private conversations as well as for relaxing (*opposite, bottom right*). This bench area provides computers so workers can access the internet; seating is in the form of high stools covered with a vibrant, lime-green fabric (*opposite, bottom left*).

The brief for the headquarters of Energinet, the Danish national energy transmission company, called for a building that emphasizes transparency and energy efficiency. Designers Hvidt & Mølgaard took inspiration for their design from the location in the rolling hills of Jutland, taking advantage of the views and responding to the open expanses of the countryside, while ensuring the structure blended into the natural environment.

The offices are broken into two distinct elements, one stacked on top of the other. The base of the building is a long rectangular structure that has been divided into various open, airy spaces. These areas are accessible to the public, and serve as a meeting place for employees and visitors. This section houses the building's entrance, reception area and central, glass-roofed atrium, all of which have been clad in Wratza, a light natural stone. Stair treads in the atrium are lined with expanded acoustic ash wood for sound absorption, and freestanding olive trees and fountains create a warm and welcoming environment.

The second element of the Energinet headquarters is a 'floating' box above the open ground floor. This space is home to the company's office facilities and offers impressive views of the landscape. To encourage collaboration between employees, café areas with a capacity for twenty-five employees are located on each floor, and have a direct visual connection with the atrium. All of the materials used in the office building's interior have been chosen to achieve a beautiful, solid and easy-to-maintain finish. Offices, meeting rooms and the main stairs therefore have light ash wood flooring. Dark, pre-patinated zinc accents lend a sculptural quality to the workspace. A central control room can be found on the second floor, but other technical facilities, as well as bathrooms, the fitness centre and the server room, have been tucked away in the basement.

Given the nature of its business, the client demanded extremely high standards of energy efficiency; this demand was also driven by Denmark's stringent regulations on levels of energy consumption permitted in new buildings. The Energinet headquarters are therefore very compact with small building surfaces in comparison to the volume of the building. It is designed to provide effective solar protection – letting in little direct sunlight, which minimizes heat gains, and also to provide effective shade for employees. The triple-glazed windows are organized in a vertical system to ensure maximum daylight, and solar cells have been installed on the south façade to augment the power supply. Efficient ventilation and provision for cooling the structure at night also contribute to the overall energy efficiency of the building.

ENERGINET HEADQUARTERS

Architect: **Hvidt & Mølgaard**
Client: **Energinet**
Location: **Fredericia, Denmark**
Completed: **December 2007**
Size: **18,220 sq m (196,120 sq ft)**
Budget: **DKR c. 250 million**

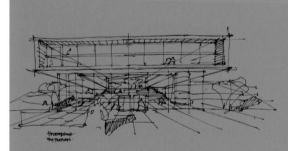

Page 296: The building has been designed to provide effective solar protection: to keep the office cool the minimum amount of direct sunlight is let in, and sufficient shade is there for the comfort of employees.

Above left: All of the materials were chosen by the designers to give a solid, light and easily maintainable finish. **Above right**: The office's many windows not only offer striking views of the landscape, but also are triple glazed to keep the heat in – a key part of saving energy. **Left**: The base of the building is a long rectangular structure, which houses the reception, atrium and meeting place for staff and visitors; on top of the base is a sort of 'floating' box, where Energinet's office facilities are.

Opposite: The ground floor has a large amount of space for employees and guests to meet (*top*). On each of the upper floors, where workspace surrounds the airy atrium that runs down the centre of the floor plan, there is café space for up to twenty-five employees (*middle* and *bottom*).

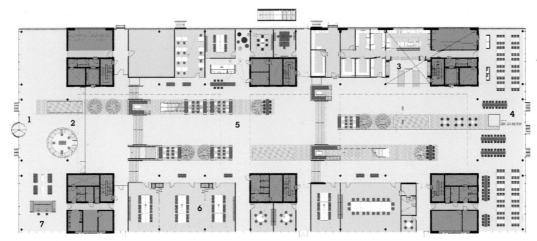

ground floor

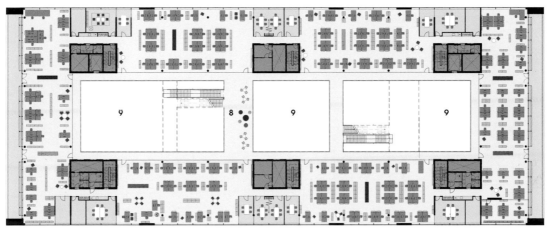

first floor

1 entrance
2 reception
3 kitchen
4 canteen
5 café/meeting
   space
6 meeting room
7 info lounge
8 café on platform
9 openings to roof

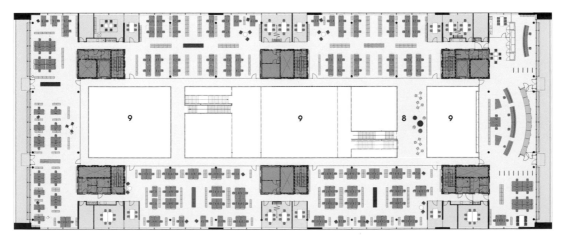

second floor

Above left: Each floor has large windows that look out over the entrance hall. The offices are therefore visually connected to the open space. **Above right**: Efficient ventilation for cooling the building means that the project meets with the client's desire for energy efficiency. **Right**: The stairs, like much of the building, are composed of light ash, a highly durable material that suits the airy aesthetic of the construction.

Opposite: Freestanding olive trees grow in the spacious atrium, helping make the atmosphere feel more warm and natural.

Architects 3XN united five separate offices of Saxo, an online investment bank, to create one purpose-built headquarters in the Danish capital. The master plan initially featured two distinct buildings, but at the client's insistence 3XN undertook a slight redesign to create a single building that looks like two structures that have been twisted, pulled apart, and put back together again.

The Saxo office is situated in the Hellerup section of Copenhagen on the former site of a Carlsberg brewery. Although it is an online bank, the company felt it was important to create an eye-catching physical presence with an architectural design that maximizes natural light. The designers took inspiration for the dramatic headquarters from Saxo's branding of itself as a dynamic, forward-looking organization. The building is shaped like two blocks with their end walls pointing towards a bordering canal. The triangle pattern, which folds around the building, is derived from the geometry of the double-curved glass and aluminium façade. The white aluminium part of the façade features panels treated with silkscreen printing and Emalit enamelled glass. These panels are intended to contrast with the transparent glass elements of the retracted façades, and they also offer an element of privacy. There are more aluminium panels on the south side of the building in order to provide adequate shading from the sun.

The interior is open and transparent and is designed to engender a sense of togetherness. The project's key aim was to create interaction and knowledge sharing throughout the company, and to this end the amount of corridors is kept to a minimum. Instead, staff are encouraged to use the stairs, and the massive staircase, located at the building's centre, is Saxo's most striking interior element: sweeping and sculptural, it spirals up to the dramatic glass-roofed atrium. A discreet glass lift placed inside the staircase offers an alternative to climbing the stairs. Fostering this community aspect, the 850-strong workforce eats together in the canteen overlooking the canal.

Situated in the upper part the building is Saxo's trading floor, where bank staff enjoy a double-height space and large windows that let the natural light flood the workspace. Above that are five executive offices on the top floor, which were designed to be modern yet cosy and provide spectacular views of the northern part of Copenhagen.

SAXO HEADQUARTERS

Architect: **3XN**
Client: **Saxo Bank**
Location: **Copenhagen, Denmark**
Completed: **August 2008**
Size: **16,000 sq m (172,220 sq ft)**
Budget: **DKR 212 million**

Page 302: The exterior, covered in polygons, appears as if it is two surfaces that have been somehow twisted apart and reassembled.

Above: The building has a clean, almost clinical, look; but the sweeping curves of the interior architecture help to make the viewer feel enclosed and engaged by their surroundings. **Left**: The stairs lead down to a glass-fronted atrium, where the transparent glass lets in plenty of natural light.

Opposite: It was important to the client that the building was eye-catching from the inside and out, so a sweeping, sculptural staircase was made the centre of the project. A glass elevator stands in the middle of the staircase and provides access for those who are unable (or unwilling) to climb the steps.

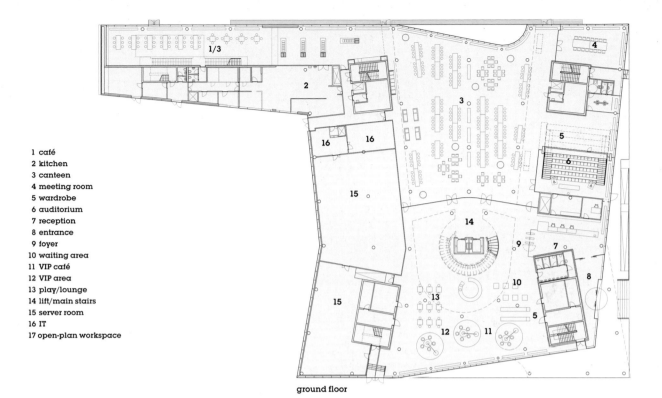

1 café
2 kitchen
3 canteen
4 meeting room
5 wardrobe
6 auditorium
7 reception
8 entrance
9 foyer
10 waiting area
11 VIP café
12 VIP area
13 play/lounge
14 lift/main stairs
15 server room
16 IT
17 open-plan workspace

ground floor

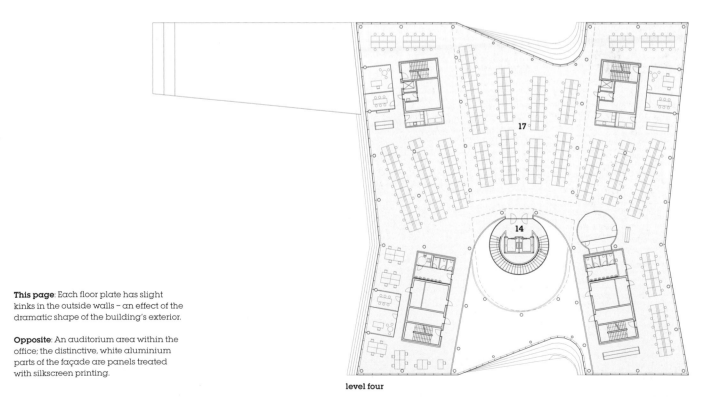

This page: Each floor plate has slight kinks in the outside walls – an effect of the dramatic shape of the building's exterior.

Opposite: An auditorium area within the office; the distinctive, white aluminium parts of the façade are panels treated with silkscreen printing.

level four

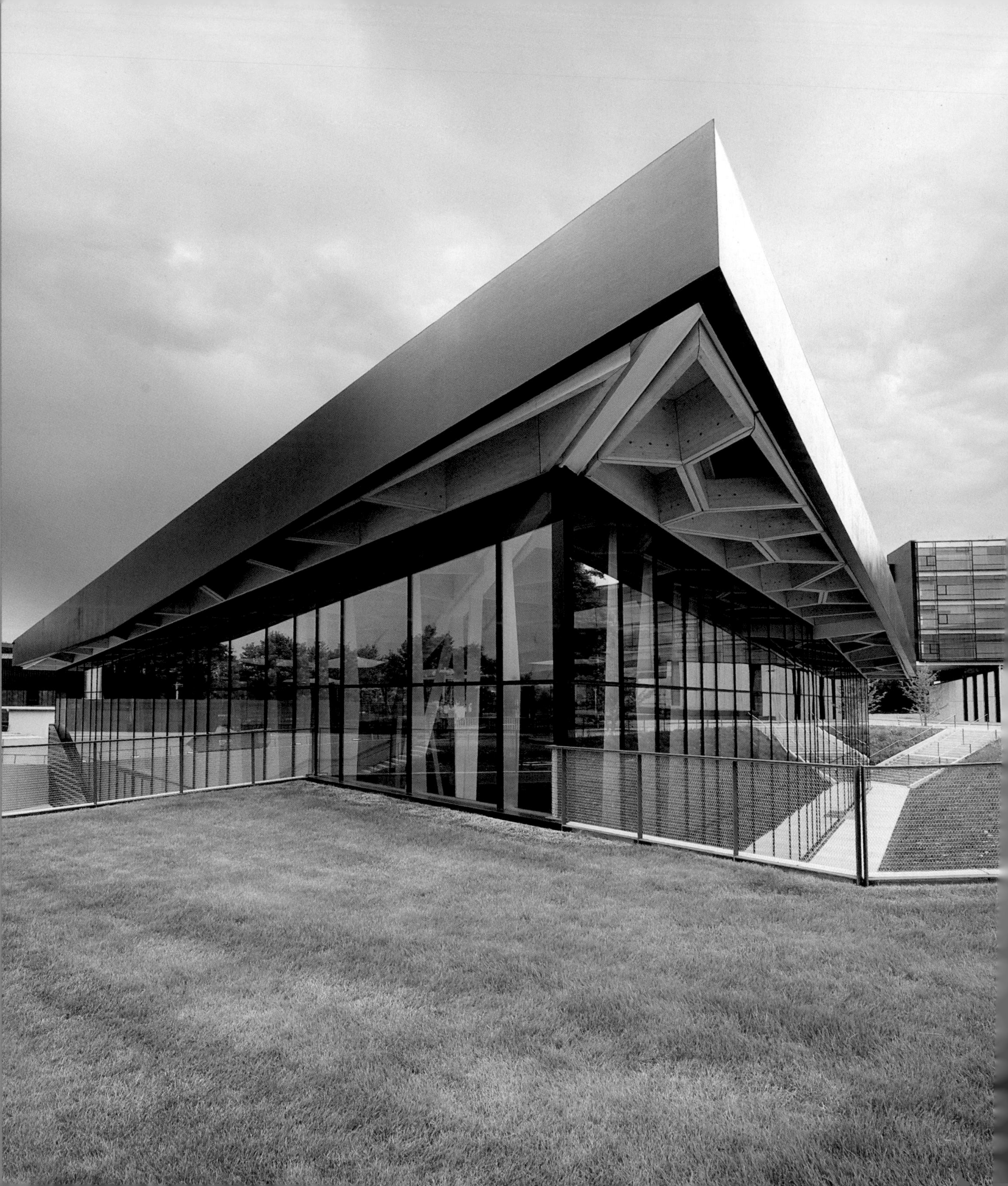

This is no ordinary office canteen, but a multifunctional hub for a laser technology firm located in the outskirts of Stuttgart. Through the resulting architecture, Berlin-based design practice Barkow Leibinger demonstrates how to use an innovative digital production process in an original way.

Located in a newly landscaped park entrance between the gatehouse and the nearby autobahn, the restaurant is at the heart of a system of spaces that lead to it. The structure connects the entire industrial campus, and its appearance is reminiscent of an excavated amphitheatre. The building has room for about 700 workers to dine, creating a sense of unity among the diverse staff, and also functions as a versatile space that can be used as an auditorium to host musical events, client presentations and lectures for up to 800 people. It is, in essence, a new social and cultural centre and its multifunctionality offsets the high cost of running a full industrial kitchen, service and storage areas. This building works hard to serve many different purposes for the company.

The restaurant's focal point is its incredible roof, which is based on a triangular structure influenced by patterns found in nature, such as leaves. The roof consists of glulam (glued and laminated timber) honeycomb – a material chosen for its sustainability – and a long-span steel structure, which was custom cut using a CNC machine. The wood acts as structural webbing between the triangular parts of the roof while the steel is splayed to give the structure stability. The honeycomb filters natural daylight through skylights, and is fitted with artificial lighting and acoustic baffles. The canteen's connection to nature is achieved via a glass façade, which wraps around the interior with sun screening courtesy of a series of rolling screens.

An extra mezzanine level has been created above the kitchen by lowering the main level of the space by 4 metres. This gives the mezzanine an air of theatricality, enhanced by the fact that it is accessed via two dramatic concrete stairways. The area is designed to accommodate overflow from the main dining area, and can be used for private conferences.

The building's crisp finishes, found everywhere from the 300 joints in the roof to the aluminium panels in the

TRUMPF EMPLOYEE RESTAURANT

Architect: **Barkow Leibinger**
Client: **Trumpf**
Location: **Ditzingen, Germany**
Completed: **July 2008**
Size: **5,400 sq m (58,130 sq ft)**
Budget: **€13.4 million**

toilet cubicles, were achieved using digitally guided tools, which can easily mass produce non-standard forms. Barkow Leibinger also developed a bespoke terracotta tile with digital tooling, and used it on both the inside and outside of the pavilion. The designers were especially excited about this element as it enabled them to produce a secondary cladding and therefore add textural interest to the geometry of the building.

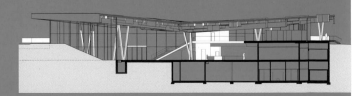

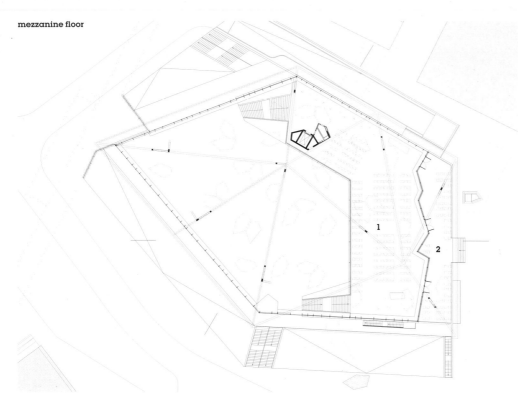

1 mezzanine café
2 terrace
3 delivery
4 storage
5 kitchen
6 serving islands
7 cafeteria/auditorium
8 entrance/tunnel connection

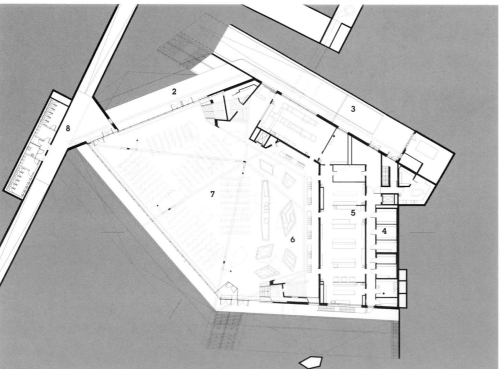

main floor

Page 308: The dramatically shaped canteen is located in a newly landscaped part of a corporate campus and functions as an events space for lectures, presentations and musical performances. The design for the roof's pointed shape took its inspiration from natural objects such as leaves.

Page 309: The restaurant is built into the ground. It is split over two levels – a main floor which is 4 metres below ground level and a mezzanine floor that is 1 metre above ground.

Above: The mezzanine level of the canteen is multifunctional – it can be used for conferences as well as dining.
Left: Furniture is arranged around the building's unusual hexagonal shape to help maximize seating capacity.

Opposite: The honeycomb structure of the ceiling is an impressive centrepiece for the restaurant. Made from glulam (glued and laminated timber) and steel, cut using a CNC cutting technique, the honeycomb structure lets in daylight through skylights and houses artificial lighting.

PROJECT LISTING

SMALL

[12] Gummo Office
Client: Gummo
Architect: i29
Project team: Jaspar Jansen,
Jeroen Dellensen
Completed: February 2009
Size: 450 sq m (4,840 sq ft)
Budget: €30,000

[18] Syzygy Office
Client: Syzygy
Architect/Design: eins:eins Architekten
Project team: Christoph Roselius, Julian
Hillenkamp, Oliver Lauber, Maren Dörfer
Completed: November 2009
Size: 368 sq m (3,960 sq ft)
Budget: undisclosed

[22] YCN Office
Client: YCN
Architect: The Klassnik Corporation
Project architect: Tomas Klassnik
Completed: April 2009
Size: 210 sq m (2,260 sq ft)
Budget: c. £40,000

[30] MORI x Hako Offices
Client: MORI x Hako
Architect: Keisuke Maeda, UID Architects
Structural engineer: Hisashi Furukawa
Contractor: Home Co.
Landscape builder: Zenjiro Hashimoto
Typography design: Makoto Ouchi
Completed: January 2009
Size: 360 sq m (3,870 sq ft)
Budget: €675,000

[38] Bearstech Headquarters
Client: Bearstech
Architect/design: Paul Coudamy
Co-design/consulting and wood structure:
Arnaud Depeyre
Assistants: Bastien Gache, Martial
Coudamy
Project manager: Pierre Brochot
Builder: Paul Coudamy
Completed: May 2009
Size: 60 sq m (650 sq ft)
Budget: undisclosed

[42] Hambly and Woolley Studio
Client: Hambly and Woolley
Architect: Cindy Rendely Architexture
Project team: Cindy Rendely
Builder: David Wyse
Completed: 2007
Size: 370 sq m (3,980 sq ft)
Budget: CAN $95,000

[46] Nothing Office
Client: Nothing
Design: Alrik Koudenburg,
Joost van Bleiswijk
Design and production:
Joost van Bleiswijk
Concept and art direction: Alrik
Koudenburg
Project management: edsonwilliams
Illustrations: Fiodor Sumkin
Completed: March 2009
Size: 100 sq m (1,080 sq ft)
Budget: €30,000

[52] TED Office
Client: TED Conferences
Architect/design: Tina Manis Associates
Project team: Tina Manis, Mandy LeBoeuf,
Brandon Kamoda
Structural consultants: Stratford
Engineering
Contractor: JAB Associates LLC
Completed: June 2008
Floor space: 310 sq m (3,300 sq ft)
Budget: US $500,000

[62] The Architecture Foundation Office
Client: The Architecture Foundation
Architect: Carmody Groarke
Project team: Kevin Carmody, Andy
Groarke, Andrew House
Completed: May 2009
Size: 170 sq m (1,800 sq ft)
Budget: undisclosed

[66] KK Outlet
Client: KesselsKramer
Architect/design: Fashion Architecture
Taste (FAT)
Contractor: John Stidworthy
Completed: December 2007
Size: 95 sq m (1,020 sq ft)
Budget: undisclosed

[72] Selgas Cano Studio
Client: Selgas Cano
Architect: Selgas Cano Arquitectos
Project team: Jose Selgas, Lucia Cano,
Jose Jaraiz (architect), Jose de Villar
(architect)
Electricity and telecommunications:
Elsues
Plumbing: Martin Juez
Wood paving and furniture: Bascope
carpenters

Completed: October 2007
Size: 60 sq m (660 sq ft)
Budget: undisclosed

[78] van der Architects Studio
Client: van der Architects
Architect: Martin van der Linden
Designers: Ayumu Ota, Nanako Tsujimoto
Project managers: Aaron McCain, Yasu Iida
Completed: August 2008
Size: 200 sq m (2,150 sq ft)
Budget: approx. 150 ml beer/sq m

MEDIUM

[84] Prisma Headquarters
Client: Prisma Engineering Maschinen- und Motorentechnik
Architect/design: SPLITTERWERK
Project team: Ellwanger, Hannes Freiszmuth, Johann Grabner, Edith Hemmrich, Ute Himmelberg, Bernhard Kargl, Benjamin Nejedly, Josef Roschitz, Maik Rost, Ingrid Somitsch, Nikolaos Zachariadis, Irene Berto, Mark Blaschitz, Erika Brunnermayer, Ernst Gschweitl
Structural consultant: werkraum, Peter Bauer, David Lemp
Building services consultant: Rudolf Sonnek
Project management: Ingenos.Gobiet.ZT
Electrical design: Erich Watzke, Moskon & Busz, Rudolf Busz
Energy consultant: Dr. Tomberger ZT GesmbH, Hannes Veitsberger
HVACR design: Günter Grabner
Completed: November 2007
Size: 1,400 sq m (15,000 sq ft)
Budget: undisclosed

[90] Moving Picture Company Office
Client: Moving Picture Company (MPC)
Architect: Patrick Tighe Architecture
Structural engineer: Gilsanz Murray Steficek
Completed: December 2009
Size: 780 sq m (8,400 sq ft)
Budget: US $1.5 million

[96] F-zein Office
Client: F-zein
Architect: klab architects
Project team: Konstantinos Labrinopoulos, Miltos Farmakis
Completed: July 2008
Size: 750 sq m (8,070 sq ft)
Budget: €90,000

[100] Digitas Office
Client: Digitas
Architect and designer: 11.04 Architects
Quantity surveyor: 11.04 Architects
Fit-out contractor: OD Projects
Specialist joiner: Koder
Completed: November 2008
Size: 1,900 sq m (20,450 sq ft)
Budget: £345,000

[106] Nestlé Latin American Headquarters
Client: Nestlé
Architect/Design: Rojkind Arquitectos, Michel Rojkind
Project team: Michel Rojkind; Rojkind Arquitectos, Agustín Pereyra and Paulina Goycoolea (project leaders), Juan Carlos Vidals (3D massing), Mónica Orozco (project management), Moritz Melchert, Tere Levy, Isaac Smeke J., Tomas Kristof, Francisco Gordillo, Andrés Altesor, Juan Pablo Espinosa
Façade engineer: VYCISA (Juan Pablo Casillas, Cybelle Hernández)
MEP and hydraulic engineer: Quantum Design
Structural engineer: Juan Felipe Heredia
Construction: SLCI Engineer José Solis
Landscape: Rojkind Arquitectos
Nestlé supervision: Flavio Guerrero, Cristian Moreno
Completed: February 2009
Size: 780 sq m (8,350 sq ft)
Budget: undisclosed

[114] Mayr-Melnhof Headquarters
Client: Mayr-Melnhof Holz Holding
Architect: Nussmüller Architekten
Interior design: Bene
Completed: November 2008
Size: 2,523 sq m (27,160 sq ft)
Budget: undisclosed

[120] Langland Offices
Client: Langland
Architect: Jump Studios
Project team: Markus Nonn, Shaun Fernandes
Contractor: The Interiors Group
Completed: December 2008
Size: 930 sq m (10,010 sq ft)
Budget: £800,000

[126] Rios Clementi Hale Studios Office
Client: Rios Clementi Hale Studios
Architect: Rios Clementi Hale Studios
Project team: Mark W. Rios, Julie Smith-Clementi, Frank Clementi, Robert Hale, Jennifer Charles, Michael Martinez
Structural engineer: Charles Tan & Associates
Contractor: Swinerton
Landscape consultant: Rios Clementi Hale Studios
Completed: December 2008
Size: 1,580 sq m (16,700 sq ft)
Budget: undisclosed

[132] Platoon Kunsthalle
Client: Platoon
Architect: Graft + Baik Jiwon
Concept design: Platoon Cultural Development
Interior design: Urbantainer
Executive architect: U-il Architects & Engineers
Prefab engineer: Ace special container
Structural engineer: MIDAS IT
Structure: M. Cabestany
Contractor: HYOJUNG Construction & Development
Completed: March 2009
Size: 920 sq m + 120 sq m roof terrace (9,910 + 1,250 sq ft)
Budget: US $2 million

[138] EDF Energy Office
Client: EDF Energy
Architect: BDGworkfutures
Mechanical and electrical services consultant: SJ Brook Consulting Engineers
Project manager and cost consultant: Leslie Clark
Contractor: Bryen & Langley
Completed: June 2009
Size: 1,800 sq m (19,380 sq ft)
Budget: undisclosed

[144] Publicmotor Office
Client: Publicmotor Brand Communication
Architect: Bottega + Ehrhardt
Project team: Giorgio Bottega, Henning Ehrhardt, Christoph Seebald
Completed: 2008
Size: 700 sq m (7,540 sq ft)
Budget: undisclosed

[150] Workspace 1212
Client: Studio Gang
Architect: Studio Gang
Project team: Jeanne Gang, Mark Schendel, Beth Kalin, Schuyler Smith

Services engineer: dbHMS (Sachin Anand)
Completed: August 2007
Size: 680 sq m (7,300 sq ft)
Budget: US $78,000

[154] Pullpo Creative Lab
Client: Gonzales Silva and Gabriel Schkolnick
Architect: Hania Stambuk
Project team: Hania Stambuk
Structural engineer: Claudio Hinojosa
Completed: 2008
Constructed area: 670 sq m (7,230 sq ft)
Budget: £150,000

[158] Geyer Office
Architect and client: Geyer Studio
Services engineer: Medland Metropolis
AV engineer: Rutledge
Building surveyor: Design Guide
Workstation design and construction: Schiavello
Completed: March 2007
Size: 560 sq m + 130 sq m deck (5,970 sq ft + 1,400 sq ft)
Budget: AUS $685,000

[162] Postpanic Office
Client: PostPanic
Architect: Maurice Mentjens Design
Project team: Maurice Mentjens, Johan Gielissen, Annet Butink
Contractor: Elan Bouwkundig Advies (Paul de Reuver)
Completed: March 2009
Size: 565 sq m (6,082 sq ft)
Budget: undisclosed

[170] bastard Store
Client: Comvert
Architect: studiometrico
Project team: Lorenzo Bini, Francesca Murialdo, Marco Lampugnani (collaborator)

Structural engineer: Atelier LC (Marco Clozza)
Quantity surveyor: studiometrico
Completed: October 2008
Floor space: 1,300 sq m (13,990 sq ft)
Budget: €2 million

[176] Billington Cartmell Office
Client: Billington Cartmell
Architect: Platform group
Completed: 2008
Size: 1,360 sq m (14,590 sq ft)
Budget: undisclosed

[182] Harmonia 57
Client: IV Incorporadora
Architect: Triptyque
Project team: Tiago Guimaraes, Greg Bousquet, Carolina Bueno, Guillaume Sibaud, Olivier Raffaelli, Laura Bigliassi, Isabella Gebara, Felipe Hess, Bob van den Brande, Flavio Miranda, Renata Pedrosa, Marc Roca Bravo, Bruno Simoes, Filipe Troncon.
Consultants: Hidraulique, HQE (Apareido Donizete Dias Flausiano and Guiherme Castanha)
Hydraulic engineer: Guiherme Castanha
Landscape consultant: Peter Webb
Completed: 2008
Size: 1,100 sq m (11,840 sq ft)
Budget: €300 million

LARGE

[190] Unilever Headquarters
Client: Hochtief for Unilever HQ
Architect/Design: Behnisch Architekten
Project team: Stefan Behnisch, David Cook, Martin Haas, Andreas Leupold, Irina Martaler, Eckart Schwerdtfeger, Dennis Wirth, Andreas Peyker, Mandana

Alimardani, Jens Berghaus, Stephan
Zemmrich (project architect), Peter Schlaier
(project leader)
Completed: September 2009
Size: 20,000 sq m (215,280 sq ft)
Budget: undisclosed

[198] **Die Futtermühle**
Client: Lorigenhof
Architect and landscape consultant:
Kaundbe Architekten
Project team: Kaundbe Architekten,
ITW Ingenieurunternehmung
Services engineer: ITW
Ingenieurunternehmung
Structural engineer: Hans Rigendinger
Quantity surveyor: atm3
Completed: Autumn 2008
Size: 2,330 sq m (25,000 sq ft)
Budget: €3.75 million

[206] **JWT Office**
Client: J. Walter Thompson Advertising
Architect: Clive Wilkinson Architects
Project team: Clive Wilkinson (design
director), John Meachem (project
manager), Neil Muntzel (project
coordinator), Hailey Soren, Lindsay Green,
Daniella Oberherr, Nicole Sylianteng,
Yana Khudyakova, Jacqueline Law
Executive architect: HOK NY:
Juliette Lam (managing principal),
Robert Kellogg (project manager),
Anthony Spagnolo (project architect),
Margaret Wells, Satomi Shimamura
Project management: WPP Group
(Joe Murphy)
Property management: Jones Lang
LaSalle: Janet Goldman,
Thomas Murray, Jeff Simpson,
Jeff Zinke, Sergio Mendes
Structural engineer: The Office
of James Ruderman
MEP consultant: Syska Hennessy

Contractor: Structuretone, GC Contracting
AV/security/telecom consultant:
Constantine Walsh-Lowe
Environmental graphics and wayfinding:
EGG Office
Fabric structures: J. Miller Canvas
Food service design: Antico Food Service
Design
Lighting: Johnson Schwinghammer
Millwork: Scanga Architectural
Woodworking, Ilan Dei Studios,
Kundig Contracting
Programming consultant: DEGW
Completed: February 2008
Size: 23,230 sq m (250,000 sq ft)
Budget: undisclosed

[216] **Department of Biochemistry, University of Oxford**
Client: University of Oxford
Architect and interior designer:
Hawkins\Brown
Design team: Russell Brown, Oliver Milton
(associate director in charge of project),
Louisa Bowles, Hazel York, Morag Morrison,
Chloe Sharpe
Services engineer: Foreman Roberts
**Structural engineer and acoustic
consultant:** Peter Brett Associates
Project management: PDCM
Contractor: Laing O'Rourke
Art consultant: Louise O'Reilly, Artpoint
Arts advisor: Paul Bonaventura, Ruskin
School of Drawing and Fine Art
Cost consultant: Turner and Townsend
Laboratory design consultant: CUH2A
Completed: October 2008
Size: 12,000 sq m (129,170 sq ft)
Budget: £49 million

[220] **Microsoft Dutch Headquarters**
Client: Microsoft
Architect: SevilPeach
Developer's architect: Cepezed

Project manager: Rietmeijer
Huisvestingsadviseurs
Lighting: Studio Rublek
Workplace consultant: Veldhoen
+ Company
Completed: August 2008
Size: 10,890 sq m (117,220 sq ft)
Budget: undisclosed

[228] **ANZ Learning Centre**
Client: ANZ Bank
Architect/design: Hassell
Project team: Robert Backhouse, Caroline
Lieu, Michael Hrysomallis, Juli Smolcic,
Darren Paul, Rebecca Trenorden, Ingrid
Bakker, Robert Harper, Nick Tennant
Building engineer: Approval Systems
Lighting engineer: NDY Light
Mechanical and hydraulics engineers:
Norman Disney & Young
Structural engineer: Connell Wagner
Quantity surveyor: Rider Hunt
Project manager: CBRE
Builder: Schiavello
Feng shui expert: Patrick Wong
Graphic designer: Fabio
Ongarato Design
Strategic brief: DEGW Asia Pacific
Completed: September 2007
Total floor space: 3,000 sq m, (32,290 ft)
Budget: undisclosed

[236] **Arts Council National Office**
Client: Arts Council England
Architect: Caruso St John
Services engineer: GDM
Structural engineer: Price & Myers
**Project manager, quantity surveyor
and planning supervisor:**
Jackson Coles
Consultant artist: Lothar Goetz
Completed: 2008
Size: 3,300 sq m (35,520 sq ft)
Budget: £3 million

[240] Potterrow Development, School of Informatics

Client: University of Edinburgh

Architect: Bennetts Associates

Design team: Doug Allard, Sarah Bangham, Rab Bennetts, Alasdair Gordon, Hamish Gunns, Tom Hayes, Anisa Hussein, Emiel Koole, David Liston, Kirsty Maguire, Iain McKenzie, John Miller, James Nelmes, Sara Oxley, Patrick Stegbauer, Sybille Stolze, Scott Wardlaw, Stuart Watson

Structural and building services engineer: Buro Happold

Fire engineer: Buro Happold

Contractor: Balfour Beatty

Landscape architect: Ironside Farrar

Acoustic consultant: New Acoustic

Cost consultant: Turner & Townsend

Completed: June 2008

Size: 16,500 sq m (177,610 sq ft)

Budget: £41.2 million

[244] Fairlands Office

Client: FNB HomeLoans and WesBank

Architect: Continuum Architects

Project team: Kim Fairburn, Karuni Naidoo, Pat Henry, Mphethi Morojele, Derek Lubbe, Vuyani Mabuto, Lemmy Khama

Mechanical engineers: Spoormakers/DTM Anton Frylinck

Engineer: Mpumelelo Engineers

Structural and civil engineers: Africon

Quantity surveyors: Pentad, Frans De Jager

Project managers: Focus Project Managers, SIP Project Managers

Contractor: Fairlands JV (WBHO and Grinaker LTA)

Completed: March 2008

Site area: 160,000 sq m (1,722,230 sq ft)

Budget: undisclosed

[254] IFAW Headquarters

Client: International Fund for Animal Welfare (IFAW)

Architect: DesignLAB

Civil engineer: Down Cape Engineering

MEP engineer: TMP Engineers

Structural engineer: Odeh Engineers

Landscape architect: Stephen Stimson Associates

Cost estimators: KVAssociates

Completed: January 2008

Size: 5,020 sq m (54,000 sq ft)

Budget: US $12.5 million

[260] SGAE Offices

Client: SGAE

Architect: Ensamble Studio

Project team: Antón García-Abril, Ensamble Studio

Collaborating architects: Débora Mesa Molina, Ricardo Sanz Soriano, Marina Otero Verzier, Elena Pérez López, José Antonio Millán Mena

Structural engineer: Jesús Huerga

Quantity surveyor: Javier Cuesta

Services engineer: Obradoiro

Builder: Materia Inorgánica

Completed: January 2007

Size: 4,000 sq m (43,060 sq ft)

Budget: €8 million

[264] Vodafone Headquarters

Client: Vodafone

Architect: Barbosa & Guimarães

Architects: José António Barbosa, Pedro Lopes Guimarães

Collaborators: Ana Campante, Ana Carvalho, Ana Mota, Daniela Teixeira, Eunice Lopes, Filipe Secca, Henrique Dias, Hugo Abreu, Nuno Felgar, José Marques, Miguel Pimenta, Pablo Rebelo, Paula Fonseca, Paulo Lima, Raul Andrade, Sara Caruso

Electrical engineer: RGA (Luis Fernandes)

Hydraulic engineer: Afaconsult (Marta Peleteiro)

Mechanical engineer: RGA (Pedro Albuquerque)

Structural engineer: Afaconsult (Carlos Quinaz)

Construction: Teixeira Duarte

Completed: November 2009

Size: 7,470 sq m (80,430 sq ft)

Budget: €11.5 million

[272] Newham Council Headquarters

Client: London Borough of Newham Council

Architect: ID:SR

Project team: Helen Beresford, Andrew German, Daniel Winder, Mel Bissett, Daniel Galleni, Sarah Bunch, Karen van Eeden, Cindy Ho, Sasha Lieven

Base-build architects: Aukett Fitzroy Robinson

Associate architect: Daniel Winder

Services engineer: Chapman Bathurst (Associate: Joe Gibson)

Structural engineer: Ramboll Whitbybird (Martin Burden and Alex Hall)

Quantity surveyor: London Borough of Newham Design Services (Liam Keaveney)

Project management: Gardiner Theobald (Miles Delap and Anne-Marie Taylor)

Design and build contractor: Overbury (Neil Solomon)

CDM coordinator: Gardiner Theobald (Paul Saward)

Completed: June 2009

Size: 23,000 sq m (247,570 sq ft)

Budget: undisclosed

[276] S11 Office Complex

Client: Cogiton Projekt Altstadt

Architect: Jürgen Mayer H.

Project team: Jürgen Mayer H., Hans Schneider, Wilko Hoffmann, Marcus Blum

Architect on site: Imhotep, Donachie

und Blomeyer, Dirk Reinisch
Structural engineer: WTM
Building services engineer: Energiehaus,
Sineplan
Model: Werk5
Completed: November 2009
Size: 3,000 sq m (32,290 sq ft)
Budget: undisclosed

[284] MTC Inversions Office
Client: MTC Inversions
Architect: bailo + rull / ADD +
ARQUITECTURA
Project team: Manuel Bailo Esteve, Rosa
Rull Bertran, A. Brito, M. Camallonga,
N. Canas, A. Estevez, N. Font, M. Girbau,
M. Hita, P. Jenni, A. Marin, A. Mañosa,
J. Maroto, Y. Olmo, J. Pala, A. Rovira, L. Troost
Engineers: Josep Mª Domenech,
Xavier Valls
Project manager: Anna Rovira
Completed: April 2008
Size: 3,580 sq m (38,500 sq ft)
Budget: €1.9 million

[288] Student Loans Company Office
Client: The Student Loans Company
Architect and interior designer: 3FOLD
Architect: Shuttleworth Picknett &
Associates
Mechanical engineer: QuinnRoss
Structural engineer: WCJ
Quantity surveyor: Faithful + Gould
Project manager and brief consultant:
tmd Building Consultancy
Contractor: Rok
Completed: June 2008
Size: 5,300 sq m (57,070 sq ft)
Budget: £8.5 million

[296] Energinet Headquarters
Client: Energinet
Architect: Hvidt & Mølgaard
Project team: Henrik Hvidt and Marius

Lorentzen (principals); Kim Thomassen
and Henrik Aabye (project leaders);
Masato Matsushita (sketch architect);
Anders Stangerup, Katrine Rose and Sven
Perdrup (project architects); Judith
Peülecke (technical assistant); Hrund
Winckler (interior architect)
Structural and services engineer: Ramboll
Quantity surveyor: Hoffmann
Landscape consultant: Kristine Jensens
Tegnestue
Completed: December 2007
Size: 18,220 sq m (196,120 sq ft)
Budget: DKR c. 250 million

[302] Saxo Headquarters
Client: Saxo Bank
Architect: 3XN
Project team: Kim Herforth Nielsen,
Bo Boje Larsen, Klaus Mikkelsen,
Flemming Tanghus, Mette Baarup, Anne
Strandgaard Hansen, Jakob Ohm Laursen,
Torsten Wang, Olaf Kunert, Esther
Clemmensen, Rikke Rützou Arnved, Esben
Trier Nielsen, Melanie Zirn, Rasmus Kruse,
Jan Ammundsen, Helge Skovsted, Allan
Brinch, Jens Martin Højrup, Esben Trier
Nielsen, Robin Vind Christiansen, Jesper
Malmkjær, Jeanette Hansen, Kasper Hertz
Services engineer: Ramboll
Structural engineer: Ramboll
Landscape architect: Land+
Completed: August 2008
Size: 16,000 sq m (172,223 sq ft)
Budget: DKR 212 million

[308] Trumpf Employee Restaurant
Client: Trumpf
Architect: Barkow Leibinger
Project team: Jason Sandy, Johanna
Doherty, Klaus Reintjes, Lukas Weder,
Philipp Heidermann, Caspar Hoesch,
Mathias Olive, Christina Moeller,
Dagmar Pelger, Jason Sandy

Climate engineer: Transsolar
Electrical engineers and lighting:
IBB Ingenieure
Structural engineer: Werner Sobek
Project management: Gassman +
Grossmann
Landscape: Buero Kiefer
HVAC: Krebs Ingenieurebüro
Completed: July 2008
Size: 5,400 sq m (58,130 sq ft)
Budget: €13.4 million

PHOTOGRAPHIC ACKNOWLEDGMENTS

Images are referred to by page number.
Key: t=top, b=bottom, l=left, r=right

SMALL

Gummo Office
i29: 4, 12, 14–15, 16

Syzygy Office
Studio Uwe Gärtner: 18, 20–21

YCN Office
Guy Archard: 22, 24, 25,26, 27, 28, 29

MORI x Hako Offices
UID Architects: 30, 32, 33, 34–35, 37

Bearstech Headquarters
Benjamin Boccas: 38, 40, 41

Hambly and Woolley Studio
Tom Arban: 42, 44, 45

Nothing Office
Joachim Baan: 46, 48, 49, 50, 51

TED Office
Francis Dzikowski (Esto photographic
agency): 52, 54, 55, 56, 57

Global Factoring Office
Amit Geron: 58, 60, 61

The Architecture Foundation Office
Richard Davies: 62, 65

KK Outlet
Timothy Soar: 66, 68–69, 70, 71

Selgas Cano Studio
Iwan Baan: 10–11, 72, 74–75, 76, 77

van der Architects Studio
van der Architects: 78, 80, 81

MEDIUM

Prisma Headquarters
Photos © Nikolaos Zachariadis:
84, 86–87, 89

The Moving Picture Company Office
Art Gray: 90, 92–93, 94

F–zein Office
Babis Loizidis: 96, 99

Digitas Office
Morley von Sternberg: 100, 102,
103, 104, 105

Nestlé Latin American Headquarters
Paúl Rivera: 106, 109, 110–11,
112, 113

Mayr-Melnhof Headquarters
Jorj Konstantinov: 82–83
Paul Ott: 114, 117, 118, 119
Images courtesy of Bene AG
Plans on 116 copyright Nussmueller
Architekten ZT GmbH

Langland Offices
Gareth Gardner: 120, 122, 124, 125

Rios Clementi Hale Studios Office
Tom Bonner: 126, 129, 130, 131

Platoon Kunsthalle
Platoon: 132, 134, 135, 136, 137

EDF Energy Office
Gareth Gardner: 138, 141, 142–43

Publicmotor Office
David Franck: 144, 146, 147, 148, 149

Workspace 1212
Steve Hall (Hedrich Blessing
Photographers): 150, 153

Pullpo Creative Lab
Marcelo Caceres: 154, 157

Geyer Office
Shannon McGrath: 158, 160, 161

PostPanic Office
Arjen Schmitz: 2–3, 162, 164, 165, 166–67,
168, 169

bastard Store
Guiliano Berarducci: 170, 172,
174, 175

Billington Cartmell Office
Gareth Gardner: 176, 178–79, 181

Harmonia 57
Beto Consorte: 185
Nelson Kon: 182, 186, 187

LARGE

Unilever Headquarters
Adam Mørk: 190, 193, 194, 196, 197

Die Futtermühle
Barbara Buegler: 198, 200
Juergen Fraenzer: 202–03,
204, 205

JWT Office
Eric Laignel: 206, 209, 210–11, 213,
214–15. Images courtesy of Clive
Wilkinson Architects

**Department of Biochemistry,
University of Oxford**
Keith Collie: 216, 219

Microsoft Dutch Headquarters
Harold Pareira: 226, 227
Gary Turnbull: 220, 223, 224, 225

ANZ Learning Centre
Earl Carter: 228, 230–31, 233,
234–35

Arts Council National Office
Hélène Binet: 236, 239

**Potterrow Development,
University of Edinburgh**
Keith Hunter: 240, 243

Fairlands Office
Michael Pawley: 244, 246–47, 248,
250–251, 252, 253

IFAW Headquarters
Peter Vanderwarker: 254,
256–257, 259

SGAE Offices
Roland Halbe: 260, 263

Vodafone Headquarters
Nelson Garrido: 264, 266–267, 269,
270–271

Newham Council Headquarters
Richard Waite: 272, 275

S11 Office Complex
David Franck: 1, 276, 278, 279, 280,
281, 283

MTC Inversions Office
José Hevia: 284, 287

Student Loans Company
Photos © Renzo Mazzolini: 288, 290,
292–293, 294–295

Energinet Headquarters
Helene Høyer Mikkelsen: 298tr
Hvidt Arkitekter: 301tl, 301br
Adam Mørk: 296, 298tl, 298bl,
300, 301tr

Saxo Headquarters
Adam Mørk: 302, 304, 305, 306

Trumpf Employee Restaurant
Amy Berkow: 188–89
David Franck: 311
Christian Richters: 308

INDEX

Page numbers in *italic* refer to illustrations.